David A. Wells

Our merchant marine, how it rose, increased, became great

David A. Wells

Our merchant marine, how it rose, increased, became great

ISBN/EAN: 9783337127336

Printed in Europe, USA, Canada, Australia, Japan

Cover: Foto ©Andreas Hilbeck / pixelio.de

More available books at **www.hansebooks.com**

1855 75.5. p.c.

1859 69.9. p.c.

1861 41.4. p.c.

1867 33.9 p.c.

1872 28.5.p.

1878 22.6.p.c.

1880 17.4.p.c.

1881 16.2.p.c.

1890 .... p.c.

Proportionate size of the flag of the American Merchant Marine to domestic export and import business covered by it, at different periods si 1855. Prospective size in 1890? See page 24.

OUR

MERCHANT MARINE

HOW IT ROSE, INCREASED, BECAME GREAT, DECLINED AND DECAYED

WITH

AN INQUIRY INTO THE CONDITIONS ESSENTIAL TO ITS RESUSCITATION AND FUTURE PROSPERITY

BY

DAVID A. WELLS

" Navigation and naval power are the children, not the parents—the effect, not the cause, of commerce." — McCulloch.

The United States treats commerce upon the ocean as an enemy to domestic industry. Great Britain fosters commerce as an aid to her home industries, and as the carrier that provides markets for her manufactures.

NEW YORK

G. P. PUTNAM'S SONS

27 AND 29 WEST 23D STREET

1890

PREFACE.

THE expulsion of the Moors and Jews from Spain under Ferdinand and Isabella and their successors, and the repeal of the " Edict of Nantes," which deprived France of her best artisans and industries, have been accepted by all historians and economists as the two most striking and exceptional examples in modern times, of great national industrial disaster and decay directly contingent on unwise and stupid, but at the same time deliberately adopted, state policies. It has been reserved for the United States, claiming to be one of the most enlightened and liberal nations of the world, after an experience of near three hundred years since the occurrence of the above precedents, to furnish a third equally striking and parallel example of results contingent on like causes, in the decay and almost annihilation of her merchant marine and ocean carrying trade, — a branch of her domestic industry which formerly, in importance, ranked second only to agriculture. It is proposed to tell, in the following pages, the story of this happening, and to endeavor to deduce from a record of sad and mortifying experience, what changes in federal statutes and national policy are essential to resuscitate and again make prosperous our shipping interest.

The narrative and arguments embodied in this volume were

iii

originally prepared at the suggestion and request of W. H. Hurl-
burt, Esq., editor of "The New-York World," and first appeared
in the columns of that journal, in the early part of 1881. As now
presented, they have been carefully revised, and in great part
re-written, and made to include the results of more recent experiences and continued investigations.

NORWICH, CONN., May, 1882.

CONTENTS.

OUR MERCHANT MARINE.

CHAPTER I.

THE PERIOD OF DEVELOPMENT AND PROSPERITY.

IT is proposed to here ask the attention of the public to a popular but comprehensive exhibit of that department of American commerce and industry which is concerned in the business of transporting, through the medium of vessels, merchandise and passengers between the United States and foreign countries; its origin and development, its present condition and causes of decay, and its possible future.

The presentation and discussion of economic questions are not matters which for the last twenty-five or thirty years have found much favor with the masses of the American people. The problem of slavery, the war, and the political and social questions involved in the reconstruction of the Confederate States, have largely preoccupied public attention during this period; while the resources of the country, the energies of our people, and their skill in the invention and application of machinery, have under ordinary conditions always and so easily

brought such large returns of material abundance as to
cause the nation to regard with almost complete indifference the existence of economic evils which in less-favored
countries would have been in a high degree obstructive
of all prosperity. In fact, the nation, in its economic
experience, may be not inaptly compared to those stalwart
specimens of manhood which, in virtue of their superb
physical constitutions, seem to be able with impunity to
set sanitary laws at defiance ; shirking no hardships or
exposures, careless in respect to nutriment, reckless in
the use of stimulants, and, in the exuberance of present
health, disposed to regard any word of warning for the
future as something for which there is no occasion. But,
though in exceptional cases there may be long delay, the
penalty of violated sanitary and economic laws alike is
always ultimately exacted : in the one case through various forms of physical disease or premature decrepitude,
and in the other through an unnecessary inequality in the
distribution of wealth, the promotion of class, sectional,
or national antagonisms, and the partial or total arrest of
national development. The denial by this nation to a
portion of its people of the freedom of their persons and
the ownership of the products of their labor, although
such denial was for a long time claimed by those interested to be economically successful, was ultimately settled
for by a vast expenditure of blood and treasure. The
continued use of bad and dishonest money after the
war — first occasioning inflation and then collapse — was

a prime factor in producing the financial revulsions of 1873, and in maintaining the subsequent five long years of commercial bankruptcy and industrial stagnation; while the long-continued national policy of restricting the free use of certain of the necessary instrumentalities of commercial exchange is at last so manifestly resulting in such a rapid and complete destruction of an industry which formerly ranked second only in importance in this country to agriculture, that the nation for the first time seems now willing to become interested and instructed, and to appreciate the necessity in this specialty of prompt remedial legislation. To discuss remedies in respect to ailments in the body politic, no less than in the body physical, before thoroughly making what in medical language is termed a diagnosis of the situation, is, however, but empiricism and quackery; and any possible resulting advantage from such a course cannot be other than accidental. Let us, therefore, in the first instance, endeavor to find out and comprehend the exact situation.

The Building and Use of Ships in North America during its Colonial Period.

The building and use of ships were employments which the founders of the North American Colonies and their descendants subsequently, until within a very recent period, may be said to have adopted naturally; and from the middle of the seventeenth until the middle of the nineteenth century — a period of two hundred years —

they were the two industries whose competition England, with good cause, especially dreaded. In fact, within little more than twenty-five years after the settlement of New England, or in 1650, the **English** Parliament, in full accord with the then spirit of the age, felt it necessary to enact a statute for the avowed purpose of protecting English shipping against the competition of the English plantations in America; which statute was followed during the next one hundred and twenty years by a series of twenty-nine further separate enactments, all tending to **the same** end, namely, restriction of colonial trade. By the statute of 1650 the export and import trade of the English Colonies was restricted to English or Colony built ships; and by the statute of 1663 nothing was allowed to be imported into a British plantation except in an English-built ship, "whereof the master and three-fourths of the **crew are English."**

But notwithstanding **these restrictions the** business of ship-building and ship-using in the American Colonies was one that **would** not **stay restricted, but continued to** grow in spite **of** all efforts of the mother country to the **contrary.** At the time of the breaking-out **of the** American Revolution, and for long afterwards, there were more people in the northern part of New England — Maine and New Hampshire — engaged in ship-building and in navigation than there were in agriculture; and Massachusetts **at** the same time was estimated to have owned one vessel for every hundred of its inhabitants. The enactment of arbitrary laws on the part of Great Britain to prevent her American colonists from freely participating in the carrying trade and commerce of the ocean was, however, a sore grievance, and ultimately, as is well known, constituted one of the prime causes of the American Revolution. They were, furthermore, from the very first either openly or secretly resisted and evaded ; and under their influence the colonists became a nation of law-breakers. Nine-tenths of their merchants were smugglers. One-quarter of all the signers of the Declaration of Independence were bred to commerce, to the command of ships, and to contraband trade. Hancock, Trumbull (Brother Jonathan), and Hamilton were all known to be cognizant of or participants in contraband transactions, and approved of them. Hancock was the prince of contraband traders, and with John Adams as his counsel was appointed for trial before the Admiralty Court in Boston, at the exact hour of the shedding of blood at Lexington, in a suit for five hundred thousand dollars penalties alleged to have been incurred by him as a smuggler.

Opinions of the Fathers, and the Original Policy of the New Republic.

The pertinency of the introduction of these historical facts in this connection, is to be found in the evidence they embody of the opinions entertained by the founders of the Republic respecting the justice or expedience of laws arbitrarily enacted for the restriction of commerce

and the freedom of trade. Men like Hancock, **Trumbull,**
and Hamilton, who **were** merchants before **they became**
statesmen, **had, as the result of** personal experience, **been**
led to feel that the Government of Great Britain, in en-
deavoring through such laws **to restrain** the colonists
from engaging freely **in a** department of otherwise lawful
industry, and from enjoying the fruits of their labors, con-
travened their natural rights, re-affirmed the principle of
slavery, and became their enemy. Every **evasion** of such
statutes was therefore, in their view, a blow **in favor** of
liberty. Hence also the origin of that count in the in-
dictment against the king of Great Britain, embodied in
the Declaration of Independence, "of cutting off our trade
with all parts of the world."

Such were the views of the men who a hundred years
ago were accounted the wisest of American patriots and
statesmen. **It is curious also to note how** subsequently
an attempt **was made, under the influence of** these
same old-time statesmen, to **incorporate the idea of** free
commerce and unrestricted trade with all **nations as a**
part **of** the fundamental and permanent policy of the
new Republic. Thus, up to the period of the American
Revolution, **treaties** of commerce between nations had
been little other than agreements to secure special and
exclusive privileges **to the** contracting parties, and to
antagonize **as far as possible the** commercial interests
of all other **countries. But in the** treaty of commerce
entered into between France and the United States

in 1778, the commissioners of the two nations — Franklin, Deane, Lee, and Gerard — evidently determined to attempt to inaugurate a more **generous** policy, and establish a precedent for freer and better commercial relations **between** different countries than had **hitherto prevailed.** **It was** accordingly agreed in the treaty in question **to** avoid "all those burdensome prejudices which are usually sources of debate, embarrassment, and discontent," **and to** take as the "basis of **their** agreement the **most** perfect equality and **reciprocity.**" And they further **stated the** principle which they had adopted as a guide **in their** negotiations **to be,** that of "founding **the advantages of** commerce solely upon reciprocal utility and the just **rules** of free intercourse." **The commissioners were, however,** ahead of their times, **as** they even yet would be, if still alive and participating in the public policy of the United States. The traditions and habits of Europe were also too strong to be at once broken down. The prevailing idea then everywhere was, that whatever of advantage one nation or country gained in trade and commerce necessarily entailed an equal and corresponding loss upon some other nation or country ; and in the end the **Americans succumbed** ; and **within a** comparatively few years **their own** country, falling **into the rut** of old prejudice, enacted **(as will be** hereafter shown) a commercial code as illiberal and narrow in most respects as any that had preceded it, and which **still stands as** the most striking, and in fact the only, relic of the unchristian and barbarous commercial

legislation which everywhere characterized the eighteenth
century.

History of the United-States Mercantile Marine subsequent to the Revolution.

At the time of the formation of the Constitution in
1789, the registered tonnage of the United States, by
which is to be understood the tonnage engaged in foreign
trade, was 123,893 tons. During the next succeeding
eight years, or from 1789 to 1797, it increased 384 per
cent; but this remarkable increase was exceptional, and
was due to the almost universal state of war in Europe,
which threw the carrying trade of the world in an equal
degree into our hands. Between 1797 and 1807 the increase was 42 per cent, or from 597,777 tons to 848,307
tons. Between 1807 and 1837 there was no increase, but
periods of decrease (as between 1811 and 1814 and 1818
and 1825) and again of partial recovery, so that in 1837
the amount of American registered tonnage was only
810,000 tons, or about 38,000 tons less than it was thirty
years previously, or in 1807. Subsequent to 1837 the increase was again rapid, rising from 810,000 in that year to
1,241,000 in 1847, to 2,463,000 in 1857, and culminating
with 2,642,000 tons in 1861, or at the period of the outbreak of the war. The maximum tonnage of the United
States at any one time, registered and enrolled (or engaged in foreign and domestic trade) and in the fisheries,
was in 1861, namely, 5,539,813 tons. The tonnage of the

world at that time, divided among the different nationalities, was also approximately as follows : —

	TONS.
Belonging to the United States	5,539,813
Belonging to Great Britain and her dependencies . .	5,895,369
Belonging to all other nations	5,800,767

The aggregate tonnage belonging to the United States in 1861 was therefore but a little smaller than that of Great Britain, and nearly as large as the entire tonnage of all maritime nations combined, with the exception of **Great Britain.** In respect to the international carrying trade of the world, the United States had more tonnage engaged than all other nations combined, exclusive of Great Britain.

Another point of great importance to **be** noted in this connection, and one which has been generally overlooked in all recent discussions of the decadence of American shipping, is that from 1855 to 1860, the period when the American shipping interest attained its greatest prosperity, the tonnage of the United States engaged in foreign trade was more than 50 per cent in excess of what would have been requisite to carry all the exports and the **imports of** the country; or, in other words, if American vessels had exclusively moved all our exports and all our imports from **1855** to 1860, there would have remained some 1,300,000 **tons of American** shipping to be other**wise** accounted **for in respect** to business. But as the American vessels did not at that time exclusively carry

all our imports and exports, and as fully 25 per cent of
the foreign trade of the United States was then done by
foreign vessels, it follows that the tonnage of the United
States in 1855–60, which was in excess of the immediate
trade requirements of the country, was much more than
1,300,000 tons.   Now, what was all this surplus tonnage
(amounting in the aggregate to more than the entire tonnage now owned by the United States and engaged in foreign trade) at that time employed about?   What was it
doing?   There is no trouble in returning an answer that
will not be disputed or in any degree questioned.   It was
earning money and profits for its owners and the country.
It was in the employment of foreigners, and engaged in a
trade with which the United States had no connection
except as a carrier.   It was flying the flag of the United
States in every part of the world where there was any
thing to buy or sell, to exchange and get gain, and was
acquiring in addition to immediate wealth the promise of
large gains for the future in that mercantile knowledge
and experience of the trade and productions of foreign
countries which practical business intercourse with them
can alone impart.   In this business it not unfrequently
happened that the American ships engaged did not return for years to their home ports ; while from 1850 to
1860 there was .not a year in which a large amount of
American   tonnage — 65,000   tons   in   1855 — was   not
transferred by sale to foreign ownership.

Attention should also be here called to the circumstance that the remarkable results as above detailed **were** achieved at a **time** when the differences in the wages of seamen, and the cost of stores, rigging, etc., on American vessels, in **favor** of their foreign competitors, were very marked, if not fully as great as at present. The expla- * nation of this anomaly is, that the crews of American **vessels,** although paid higher wages than the seamen of any other nationalities, were more efficient; consequently fewer men were needed, which reduced the cost and risk of navigation, and this last in turn reduced the cost **of** insurance, as compared with English **ships,** even **in** English companies. The **Americans, also,** very **early** introduced labor-saving machines and **mechanism, as for** managing the top-sails, handling **and lifting the anchor,** loading **and** unloading **freights, which also largely dis-** **pensed with the necessity of manual labor.** In a report recently made (1880) to the Legislature of Massachusetts by the Harbor Commissioners of Boston, **attention is** called to the circumstance that **even now the method of** **procedure in** unloading **vessels at American wharves is** greatly superior to that **followed in the famous docks of** London **and** Liverpool, **and as involving especially less** manual labor.[1] **Vessels of the United States at the time**

---

[1] When I landed at Liverpool, the engineer of the Mersey Docks told me that in the handling **of goods America had little to learn in Europe,** and that he had sent his **assistant to** America, **last** year, to examine **our** system of handling goods, in order that **he might** introduce in his new docks and ware-houses, now building in Liverpool, all American improvements. Still he said

under consideration were better modelled, and, **being**
better modelled and better handled, they sailed faster,
and as a general rule could make four voyages while the
Englishman under similar circumstances and with similar
vessels could make but three. American ship-owners consequently obtained more freight and often better prices,
— a sixteenth of a penny more per pound, for example,
in cotton ; and in English ports, other things being equal,
English merchants preferred to ship in American rather
than in British bottoms. In 1857, when the rebellion **in**
India broke out, and the British Government found it
necessary to despatch troops and stores with the **greatest**

---

there was one thing in which Europe was in advance of America, and **that**
was the use of hydraulic machinery. This I found to be true, and **no dock**
visited was found without large hydraulic engines and hydraulic cranes.
But it was laughable at times to see how goods were handled so carefully, so
easily, and so cheaply, by this splendid machinery, and then to see the whole
saving **wasted.   For instance, at Antwerp a vessel with broken** pig-iron was
being discharged **by one of the beautiful hydraulic swinging cranes** of Sir
William Armstrong. The **iron was hoisted from the hold in** a large tub,
which, instead of being swung over to the car standing upon the track only
fifteen feet away, and then dumped, was lowered to the deck, and then the
iron was handled piece by piece, and placed in a basket, the basket placed
upon a man's shoulder, and the man walked down a plank **to** the dock, up
another plank **on** the farther side **of the** car, and then dumped his basket
into the car.   It was in vain to ask why the tub was not swung and then
dumped, — they **never did it so.**

   In London, with a hydraulic crane lying idle alongside the ship, bale goods
were rolled from the car down to the pier, and then rolled up again to the
vessel's deck. To the question, " Why do **you do so?"** the answer was,
" We always have." — *Report W. P. Phillips, 1881.*

promptitude, the vessels that were first chartered, at the highest prices, which were most relied upon, and did the best service, were the magnificent American-built clippers at that time largely engaged in the India and China trade.

The fact here noted, namely, that under apparently the most adverse circumstances the ships of the United States engaged in foreign trade were achieving the most marked success over all foreign competitors, also long ago attracted the attention of Daniel Webster; and in a speech in opposition to one of Mr. Clay's protective tariff bills, he made use of the following language : —

"If any thing should strike us with astonishment," he said, "it is that the navigation of the United States should be able to sustain itself. Without any government protection whatever, it goes abroad to challenge competition with the whole world; and in spite of all obstacles it has yet been able to maintain eight hundred thousand tons in the employment of foreign trade. How, sir, do ship-owners and navigators accomplish this? How is it that they are able to meet, and in some measure to overcome, universal competition? It is not, sir, by protection and bounties, but by unwearied exertion, by extreme economy, by unshaken perseverance, by that manly and resolute spirit which relies on itself to protect itself. These causes alone enable American ships still to keep their element and show the flag of their country in distant seas. But when we consider that the articles entering into the composition of a ship, with the exception of wood, are dearer here than in other countries, we cannot but be utterly surprised that the shipping interest has been able to sustain itself at all."

In making this statement Mr. Webster clearly expressed the exact situation; and, with this record of remarkable

success under great difficulties, it seems clear that the
more remarkable decadence which has since befallen the
American shipping interest cannot be rightfully referred
to natural causes, but must be the result of artificial
agencies, and, therefore, within the province of remedy.

This curious condition of affairs has also not escaped
the attention of foreign investigators in this department
of economic history; and Mr. W. S. Lindsay, in his
"History of Merchant Shipping" (London, 1876), thus
comments upon it : —

"When, towards the close of the war of independence, the struggle
for supremacy commenced, the shipping of both England and America
was under the leading-strings of their respective legislators. England
would not then allow American vessels to trade with most of her vast
possessions, and, while thus nursing her ship-owners, prevented the
mass of her people from deriving the advantages invariably flowing
from a natural and wholesome competition. Nor did she, indeed,
confer any real benefit on this favored class: on the contrary, she
taught them to lean on protection instead of depending on their own
skill and industry. The consequences were apparent in even the
earlier results of the struggle. Having ample fields for employment
exclusively their own, English ship-owners did not enter with their
wonted energy into the direct carrying trade between their own country and America, which was so rapidly developed after the Americans
had become independent: they remained satisfied with those branches
of commerce expressly secured to them by law, and did not care to
continue their vessels in the trade with America in a competition, on
equal terms, with those of that country, especially when they found
they would have to produce a superior class of vessels, and to use
extra exertions, to make this trade pay as well as did their protected

branches of over-sea commerce without the additional **trouble of im-**
provements. It was **otherwise** with the shipping of the United States,
for there was then no other branch of **over-sea** trade where **the laws**
of nations **allowed** them to compete **on equal terms with foreign**
vessels."

"Although possessing the advantage **of vast forests of lumber, the**
American ship-builders were obliged to import **their** iron from **Great**
Britain, their hemp from Russia, and **many** other articles necessary
for their equipment from other and distant countries : they **did not,**
therefore, especially as skilled labor was higher **at** home than **in**
Europe, engage in the struggle with any special advantages ; but, being
equal in energy and industry, they had **the** incalculable advantage of
being obliged to **depend** on themselves. They **consequently** set to
work to construct that description **of** merchant-vessel likely to yield
the most remunerative returns, adopting the best **mechanical contriv-**
ances within **their reach so as to reduce navigation to the smallest**
cost consistent **with safety and** efficiency. And the **world soon saw**
the results of their **labors in their** celebrated 'Baltimore clippers,'
and **the** still more celebrated 'American liners,' which **for a** considerable period almost monopolized the carrying trade between **Great**
Britain and the United States.

"Yet, strange to say, though the superiority of the merchant-ves-
sels of the United States **soon became only** too apparent, scarcely any
improvements were adopted by Great Britain, or, indeed, by any other
nation, until wiser statesmen than had hitherto guided the councils of
this country swept away **the** whole paraphernalia of her navigation
laws, and left the **ship-owners** to rely entirely **on** their own resources.
This superiority **consisted** mainly in **the fact** that **American** ships
could sail faster, and carry more cargo in proportion to their registered tonnage, than those of their competitors. But their improvements did not rest here. In considering the expenses of a merchant-
man, manual labor is one of the most important items : and herein our

competitors, by means of improved blocks and various other mechanical appliances, so materially reduced the number of hands, that twenty seamen in an American sailing-ship could do as much work, and probably with more ease to themselves, than thirty in a British vessel of similar size. With such ships we failed to compete."

Origin and Development of the Ocean Steam-Marine of the United States.

The statistics of our shipping thus far presented have not discriminated between sailing-vessels and steamers. But there is a point just here of no little importance as throwing light on what subsequently happened. It is this. British foreign steam-shipping practically dates from 1838, when the "Sirius" and "Great Western," the two pioneer vessels, crossed the Atlantic to New York. The increase in this department was at first very slow ; and thirteen years later, or in 1851, the total British steam-tonnage engaged in foreign trade was only 65,921 tons. The foreign steam-shipping of the United States may be said to date from 1848, when it amounted to about 16,000 tons. For a number of years next subsequent, its increase was so rapid that in 1851 the foreign steam-tonnage of the United States and Great Britain were almost equal ; that of the former being 62,390 tons, and that of the latter 65,921 tons. During the single year 1849–50 we increased our ocean steam-tonnage 113 per cent ; and the sea-going qualities and performances of our vessels were so admirable, that the Cunard Company, which had then been in operation ten years, was obliged to bring out new ships to compete with them. The prospect, therefore, at one time was that the United States, although late in the start in this new department of foreign shipping, would soon equal, if not overtake, her great commercial competitor. And after 1851 the American growth steadily continued down to 1855, when our aggregate steam-tonnage engaged in foreign trade amounted to 115,000 tons. But from that time there was no more immediate progress, but a retrograde movement; so that in 1862 the aggregate foreign steam-commerce of the United States was less by 2,000 tons than it was in 1855. But even before the outbreak of the war, or in 1860–61, "there were no ocean mail-steamers, away from our own coasts, anywhere on the globe under the American flag, except, perhaps, on the route between New York and Havre, where two steamships may then have been in commission, which, however, were soon afterwards withdrawn. The two or three steamship-companies which had been in existence in New York had either failed or abandoned the business; and the entire mail, passenger, and freight traffic between Great Britain and the United States, so far as this was carried on by steam, was controlled then (as it mainly is now) by British companies." [1] After the war our foreign steam-tonnage revived a little, and amounted to 221,939 tons in 1869; since when it has every year grown smaller and smaller, and for the year 1880 was 145,604 tons.

---

[1] Hamilton A. Hill: Report to the United States National Board of Trade. 1863.

Progressive Decadence of the Merchant Marine of the United States subsequent to 1855.

· The year 1855 further marks a great natural division in the history of the entire foreign mercantile marine and ship-building industry of the United States. The record thus far is substantially a record of most remarkable progress and prosperity. The record hereafter is to be a record of decadence and disaster, which, considering the magnitude of the capital and interests involved, is almost without a parallel in the history of modern civilization.

What has happened in the twenty-seven years that have now elapsed since 1855 may be best realized by the following statistical statements : Our aggregate tonnage of every description — registered and enrolled, sail and steam, employed upon the ocean, upon the lakes, upon our rivers and harbors — has declined from 5,539,813 tons in 1861, to 4,057,734 in 1881, — a reduction of nearly 27 per cent.

Our tonnage engaged in foreign trade has declined during the same period from 2,496,894 tons to 1,335,586, a reduction of over 54 per cent.

The aggregate of tonnage of every description built in the United States in 1855 was 583,450; in 1861, 233,194 tons ; and, in 1880, 157,409 tons, — a reduction in annual increment since 1855 of 73 per cent, and since 1861 of 32 per cent. How rapidly, furthermore, this former great branch of American industry is decaying, may be also illustrated by the statement that the American tonnage built in 1880 was 35,622 less than in 1879, and 78,095 tons less than in 1878. There was a falling-off in the shipbuilding of the New England States during 1880, of 9,500 tons as compared with 1879, 44,012 tons as compared with 1878, and 105,123 as compared with 1875; while for our entire seaboard — Atlantic, Gulf, and Pacific — the tonnage built in 1880 was 142,755 tons less than the product of 1875. For the year 1881, the record as compared with that of 1880 shows that the progress of decay still continues, and is as follows: decrease in the total tonnage of the country, 10,299 tons; decrease in the number of vessels engaged in foreign trade 52, and in tonnage 17,224. In respect to vessels engaged in the coasting trade and fisheries, there were 595 less number of vessels employed, but an increase of 6,924 tons. In the cod and mackerel fisheries there was a decrease of 203 in the number of vessels, and of 1,402 in tonnage. In the whale-fishery there was no increase or decrease reported in respect to either number of vessels or tonnage. There was a decrease in sailing-tonnage of 15,866, but an increase of 53,440 tons in steam-tonnage. The amount of new tonnage constructed in 1881 was 123,048 greater than in 1880, or a total of 280,458 in 1881 as compared with 157,400 in 1880; but of this increase 61,578 was credited to canal-boat and barge constructions. The construction of one iron sailing-vessel of 36 tons was reported, and of 28,319 new iron steam-tonnage; a gain of 1,359 tons as compared with the construction of 1879, and a loss of 4,778 as compared with the results of 1874.

CHAPTER II.

THE PERIOD OF DECADENCE.

The Decadence of American Shipping not coincident with, nor occasioned by, the War.

THE decline in American ship-building and in the American carrying trade upon the ocean did not, as is popularly supposed, commence with the war, and was not occasioned by the depredations of the Confederate cruisers. These agencies simply helped on a decadence that had previously commenced, and which probably would have progressed just as far as it now has, had no war intervened. The first symptoms of the decadence appeared in 1856, in the falling-off in the sales of American tonnage to foreigners; the reduction being from 65,000 in 1855 to 42,000 in 1856, to 26,000 in 1858, and to 17,000 in 1860. During the war, however, the transfers of American tonnage to foreign flags again increased very largely, and, for the years 1862 to 1865 inclusive, amounted to the large aggregate of 824,652 tons, or to more than one-fourth of all the registered tonnage (the tonnage engaged in foreign trade) of the United States in 1860. But these transfers, it is well understood, were not in the nature of ordinary business, but for the sake of obtaining a more complete immunity from destruction upon the high seas than the United States at that time was able to afford.

The year 1856 also marks the time when the growth of our foreign steam-shipping was arrested, and a retrograde movement inaugurated; so that, as before stated, our aggregate tonnage in this department was 1,000 tons less in 1862 than it was in 1855.

The total tonnage of every description built in the United States also declined from 583,450 tons in 1855 (the largest amount ever built in any one year) to 469,393 in 1856, 378,804 in 1857, and 212,892 in 1860, a reduction of 68 per cent in five years.

During the year 1855, American vessels carried 75.6 per cent of the value of the exports and imports of the United States. After 1855 this proportion steadily declined to 75.2 per cent in 1856, 70.5 in 1857, 66.9 in 1859, and 65.2 in 1861, the year of the outbreak of the war.[1]

Notwithstanding this, the records of the United States Treasury Department show that the aggregate of Ameri-

---

[1] The assertion is sometimes made, that the origin of the decay of the mercantile marine of the United States is due in part to the reduction of the tariff in July, 1857; but there is not the slightest ground for any such supposition. The decadence in question, as above demonstrated, commenced two years previously; and, although there was a commercial depression and revulsion in 1857, it was due mainly to excessive railroad construction, and was not of long duration; and the succeeding three years, or from 1858 to 1860 inclusive, were among the most prosperous years in the history of the country.

can tonnage engaged in foreign trade and the **total** aggregate of the entire mercantile marine of the United **States**
were **greater in** 1861 **than at** any former period.   Whether
it was at this latter date all profitably employed, as it certainly was at an earlier period, cannot now be affirmed.

But the changes which have taken place within the last
twenty-six years in the ocean carrying **trade** of the United
States constitute **by far** the most striking illustrations of
the tremendous decadence and wreck which **our** foreign
maritime commerce and commercial marine have **within**
that period experienced.   During the whole period between 1855 and 1860 there was, as before noticed, **at least**
a million and **a** half of American tonnage exclusively **in**
foreign employ; "carrying cargoes from foreign ports **to**
foreign ports, for foreigners, to be used by foreigners,
and in which business Americans had no direct interest
but to receive their freight money, to **be** sent home and
added to the productive capital **of** the country."   **Of** this
great and profitable business a small proportion probably
yet remains, but how **much it is** difficult to state with
accuracy.

But let us next look **fairly** and squarely **at** another,
even **more** discouraging picture.   In 1855, of the **total**
value of all the exports from and **of** all the imports into
the United States, the American commercial marine transported **75.5** per cent.   **The record of the experience of**
the twenty-six **years that have since elapsed** may be presented in the **form of a table, and** also illustrated pictori-

ally. We ask the reader to take a good long look at the first, and not allow himself or herself to be repelled by the array of figures, for nothing like it is to be found in American history.

Percentage Exports and Imports carried in Vessels of the United States from 1855 to 1882.

YEARS.	PER CENT.
1856	75.2
1857	70.5
1859	66.9
1861	65.2
1863	41.4
1865	27.7
1867	33.9
1870	35.6
1872	28.5
1874	26.7
1878	25.9
1879	22.6
1880	17.6
1881	16.2

Or, to sum up in a few words, of the goods, wares, and merchandise exported and imported into the United States during the fiscal year 1881, American vessels transported only 16.2 per cent, and foreign vessels 83.8 per cent.

Again: If the flag of the Union, as borne by the commercial marine of the United States on the high seas,

had shrunk during the past twenty-six years in proportion
to the shrinkage of the domestic export and import business which it formerly covered, the size of the flag at different periods since 1855 would find representation in the
accompanying diagrams. (*See Frontispiece.*)

But, startling as are these figures and results, and por-
tending as they do unmistakably the almost complete
disappearance of the flag of the United States from the
ocean, they fail to convey the exact truth of the situation.
For it is to be borne in mind, that, while the business of
our shipping has been rapidly disappearing, the opportunities for business have at the same time been increasing
in a far more rapid ratio (the increase in the international
commerce of the globe between 1850 and 1880 being
estimated as high as 240 per cent) ; or, to put the case
differently, while there never was so much business calling
for the employment of merchant vessels in the history of
the world as at the present time, the extent to which the
capital and industry of the United States participate in
this business is annually growing less and less. Thus,
taking merely the trade of the United States as an example, we find that out of a total value of exports and
imports in 1860 of $762,000,000, the value transported in
American vessels was $507,000,000, or 66.5 per cent ; but
in 1881, out of a total value of exports and imports of
$1,676,636,000, American vessels transported a value of
but $268,080,000, or 15.2 per cent, a little more than one-
half of what was done twenty-two years ago, or in 1860 ;

whereas the value of the commodities transported in foreign vessels was more than six times as great in 1881 as in 1860.

Increase of Foreign Tonnage engaged in Trade with the United States since 1860.

Of the enormous increase in the foreign commerce of the United States since 1860, as above noted, every maritime nation of any note, with the exception of the United States, has taken a share. American tonnage alone exhibits a decrease. Thus, comparing 1880 with 1856, the foreign tonnage entering the seaports of the United States increased nearly eleven millions of tons; whereas the American tonnage entered during the same period exhibits a decrease of over 65,000 tons. British tonnage increased its proportion from 935,000 tons in 1856 to 7,903,000 in 1880; Germany, during the same time, from 166,000 to 1,089,000; and Sweden and Norway from 20,662 to 1,234,000. Austria, limited to almost a single seaport, jumped up from 1,477 tons in 1856 to 206,000 tons in 1880, and had, in 1879, 179 large-class sailing-vessels engaged in the American trade.

Sleepy Portugal increased during the same period from 4,727 tons to 24,449 tons. Spain, distracted with intestine feuds and dragged down with debt and taxation, increased from 62,813 tons in 1856 to 227,496 in 1880; while Russia, whose vessels participated in our trade in 1856 to the extent of only 40 tons, in 1880 reported 104,049 tons.

. During the year 1881, there was shipped **from** New York to Europe, grain to the extent of 72,276,000 bushels; *but not one solitary bushel* of this enormous quantity found transportation in an American vessel. In 1880 we did carry 1,328,436 bushels, out of a total of 113,343,163 bushels, but in 1881 not a bushel. In 1880 there were seven nationalities — Danish, Dutch, French, Portuguese, Russian, Spanish, and Swedish — that carried less than we did; but in 1881 they all outstripped us, and left us without even a place on the list. Of this shipment, British vessels carried 62 per cent. Italy took the *second* place, carrying over 5,000,000 bushels; Belgium stood *third* on the list, Norway *fourth*, Germany *fifth*, and Austria *sixth*.

*Comparative Exhibit of the Present Condition of the Industries of Ship-building **and** Ship-using in the United States and Other Countries.*

As already stated, the tonnage of the United States (including coasting, inland, and fisheries) in 1861 was only a little less than that of Great Britain, — namely, 5,539,000 and 5,895,000 respectively. For the **year** 1881, the aggregate tonnage of the United States was 4,057,-734, as compared with 4,068,034 in 1880. Of this aggregate for 1881, 1,057,430 was employed on the Northern lakes and Western rivers; 442,000 was canal-boats and barges, and 64,947 was licensed and under 20 tons. The tonnage engaged in foreign trade in 1881 was 1,335,000, as compared with 2,496,000 in 1861; and in the coasting-trade, 2,657,000 in 1881, as compared with 2,704,000 in 1861; the exclusive privileges granted by our navigation laws to this department of our industry not having sufficed to even enable it to hold its own.

The officially registered tonnage of Great Britain for the year 1880 was 6,574,513; but the aggregate tonnage of the mercantile marine that carries the British flag is estimated at a much higher figure, — 16,000,000, according to some authorities. Of sailing-vessels, Great Britain registered in 1880, 19,938; and is estimated to own more than one-third of the ocean sailing-vessel tonnage of the world. Of the steam-marine of the world, Great Britain is estimated to own sixty-three per cent, registering, in 1880, 5,247 vessels, with an aggregate tonnage of 2,723,468. To appreciate the significance of these figures it is necessary to bear in mind, that, in the case of every new steamship, the increase in the instrumentalities of commerce is to be measured, not so much by the single item of its tonnage, as by its carrying power; and that, with the same amount of tonnage capacity, the carrying power of a steamer is estimated, on an average, at fourfold that of a sailing-vessel. The 2,723,000 steam-tonnage of Great Britain, therefore, really represents, according to the old standard, 10,892,000 tons. In 1880 the United States had only 146,604 steam-tonnage, iron and wood, engaged in the foreign carrying trade of the ocean; or 75,000 tons less than in 1868.

The tonnage of iron vessels — sail and steam — built in

the United States during the six years from 1876 to 1881
inclusive amounted to only 127,298 tons ; and this trifling
amount was almost entirely for our coastwise or home
trade, in which no foreign competition whatever is allowed under the provisions of our navigation laws.   No
iron sailing-vessels were built in the United States between 1871 and 1880 ; but during the years 1880 and 1881
a construction of 44 and 36 tons respectively was officially
reported.   The total tonnage of all the iron vessels in the
United States in 1880, exclusive of barges, was 263,637 ;
embracing 4 iron sailing-ships, of 2,168 tonnage, and 325
iron steam-vessels of 261,469 tonnage.   Of this iron
steam-tonnage, only 34 vessels, of 70,640 aggregate tonnage, were engaged in foreign trade.

On the other hand, the tonnage of the iron vessels built
in Great Britain during the six years from 1876 to 1881,
inclusive, was in excess of 2,000,000 tons ; and every year
exhibits an increase in the amount of such constructions.
For the year 1881, the "out-turn" of new ships in Great
Britain was reported at over 600,000 tons gross.   On the
31st of December, 1881, the tonnage then under construction was the largest ever reported ; viz., 515 steamers, with
a total tonnage of 958,377, and 127 sailing-ships, with a
tonnage of 130,440.

More than eighty steamers of 3,000 tons and upwards
were in construction at one time in the course of the year
1881.   Every shipyard in the United Kingdom, capable
of supplying orders, was fully employed ; and prices,

simply by reason of the inability of builders to meet the demands made upon them, considerably advanced. Moss & Co., the leading British ship-reporters, close their circular for December, 1880, with this remark : " Altogether, we know no industry so fairly remunerative all round as modern-built steamers." Attention should here also be called to the circumstance that the orders on British ship-yards for these new constructions come from almost every maritime nationality in Europe, except Norway and Sweden (which, as a rule, still adhere to wooden vessels of moderate size), and even from China and Japan. With the exception of the United States, Italy, and Spain, all the maritime nations of the world are rapidly increasing their mercantile steam-marine, and the pecuniary returns of the business of recent years are considered as fully warranting the continued additions.

The following are some of the latest *reported* results : —

The German mercantile marine, although entering the field of competition at a comparatively late period, and when apparently every route of advantage had been pre-occupied by Great Britain, has been highly successful. For the year 1881, the Hamburg-American line of steam-ers is reported to have paid 10 per cent dividends on its stock, and to have also largely augmented its surplus. The Hamburg South-American line paid a dividend in 1880, of 10 per cent, and was obliged to charter an addi-tional steamer in 1881, in order to accommodate its in-creased business. The Hamburg steamship-line to China,

consisting of nine vessels, is reported as paying 11 per
cent dividends, with its shares quoted at 158. A new
steamship-line from Hamburg to the west coast of Africa
will commence to run regularly during the current year.
The increase in the freight movement of Hamburg for the
year 1881 was 25 per cent to the Pacific coast of South
America, 22 per cent to China, and 17 per cent to Brazil
and La Plata.

The fiscal report of the Cunard Company for 1880 shows
net earnings sufficient to provide for all interest, depreciation, and insurance of vessels, and a dividend on its stock
of 6 per cent per annum ; which is far better than the average return from most investments in government and railway stocks and securities. We have, therefore, in this
record a sufficient answer to the assertion so frequently
made in the United States, "that there is no money in the
ocean carrying trade, and therefore it is not worth while
for Americans to attempt to participate in it."

With the commencement of the present year (1882), a
new line of steamers has been started by the Austro-Hun-
garian Lloyds — a company which already employs some
eighty vessels, mainly in the East India trade — to run between Trieste, New York, and Brazil ; and since the with-
drawal of the " Roach " (United-States) solitary monthly
steamer between New York and Brazil, two lines of steamers, carrying the British flag, have come on in its place,
carrying merchandise at lower charges and the mails as
promptly and more frequently.

Holland is rapidly increasing her ocean steam-marine; and especially strengthening its line between Amsterdam and Java and Sumatra, by the addition of new and larger vessels.

Although it has been generally assumed that Greece, in view of its population, resources, and position, has considerably more than its proportion of the world's carrying trade, yet the Greeks themselves appear to have acquired a sudden conviction that greater maritime expansion is indispensable to their national development. Two large steamship companies are accordingly now forming in Greece, for participation in the South American and East India trade; the proprietorship and management of which it is proposed shall be entirely national, and which shall enter into direct competition with all other foreign flags. And with a view of further directly encouraging Greek vessels to engage in foreign trade, it is proposed to pay premiums on voyages to South America and the East Indies, to suppress all consular fees, to prevent consuls from having any interest in salvage cases, to introduce improvements in harbor regulations for the more speedy despatch of vessels, and to further enlarge and encourage schools of navigation.

But the most notable event in the recent experiences of the world's merchant-marine is the appearance of the Chinese in the field of competition, and the marked success which has thus far attended their undertakings in this department of productive industry. Ten years ago the

China Merchants' "Steam Navigation Company" started
with two small steamers in the coasting and river trade of
that country, and relying for the most part on borrowed
capital. It has now a fleet of 28 steamers, of 20,000 tons
carrying capacity, and a capital of 2,600,000 taels ($5,250,-
000), on which the net profits for 1880 are reported to have
been 21 per cent. Encouraged by this success, this company have during the past year, and as preliminary to the
establishment of regular lines, despatched steamers, with
officers and crews composed entirely of Chinese, to the
Sandwich Islands, to San Francisco, and to London ; and it
is not at all improbable, but on the contrary almost certain,
that within the next ten years the "Dragon flag" of the
Celestial Empire will be as familiar to the eye in our own
harbors, as that of the various European nationalities.
The Chinese commercial fleet, thus far, is almost exclusively of "British build;" but during the past year an
iron vessel for the Chinese imperial navy has been constructed in Germany. That the Chinese in the immediate
future are likely to be large purchasers of vessels and
machinery from foreign nations, is also extremely probable ; but that the United States, in view of its policy
toward the Chinese, would be likely to obtain any share in
this business, even if our shipyards and mechanics were
prepared for it, is, to say the least, very doubtful.

The one European nation whose commercial marine exhibits a decadence in any degree comparable with that
experienced by the United States is Italy ; and the causes

operative to decay, as will be hereafter shown, are essentially the same in both cases. Between 1869 and 1879, the decrease in Italian ship-building was officially reported at 80 per cent; and during the same period, no fewer than 50,-000 men connected with Italian ship-building and navigation were obliged to seek other employments. The exports and imports of Italy under the Italian flag are also steadily decreasing; and in the year 1879 alone, the effective strength of the Italian mercantile marine was diminished to the extent of 529 vessels, representing an aggregate of 23,385 tons.

As regards France, there seems to be a natural incapacity of that nation to successfully compete for any large share of the ocean carrying trade; and the amount of tonnage of all classes of vessels turned out by the French shipyards during recent years, has been comparatively small. With a view, however, of changing the situation, the French government have within the last year (1880–81) instituted a most extensive system of bounties for the development of its shipping interests. What may be the ultimate result of this policy cannot, as yet, be definitely predicted; but it is at least safe to affirm that the present supremacy which Great Britain now enjoys, of the ocean carrying trade, cannot be materially injured by any competition which needs adventitious aid in order to simply exist.

The Losses contingent upon the Decay of our Merchant Marine.

From this review of the situation, some general idea can be obtained of the losses, direct and indirect, which the United States has sustained within the last twenty-five years in the great department of domestic industry under consideration as measured, in ship-building and in the business for which ships are constructed and used. Let us next endeavor to gauge the amount of these losses as measured in money. And, *first*, as respects the business of ship-building and ship-repairing.

In 1855 the amount expended in the United States in the construction of new vessels was estimated at about $25,000,000 per annum ; and a sum considerably in excess of this for the repair and rebuilding of old vessels ; or a total for this branch of domestic industry of from $55,000,000 to $60,000,000 per annum. The bulk of this large expenditure was very largely for the labor of construction. A present annual expenditure in the United States of $25,000,000 for similar purposes would probably be an over rather than an under estimate. We start off in the money account, therefore, with a loss to the industry and business of the country, in the two items of ship-building and ship-repairing, of from $30,000,000 to $35,000,000 per annum.

Attention is next asked to the losses contingent upon our abandonment of the ocean carrying trade.

The business of transporting merchandise or **passen-**
gers by land or **by sea** is as much a productive industry
as the raising of wheat, the spinning of fibres, or the
smelting **or** forging of iron. It adds to human comfort, it
supplies wants, makes values, increases abundance. We
compass the land for opportunities for the employment of
labor and for markets for the product of labor ; and we
hold that civilization, national power, and national wealth
depend on the success with which these ends are profitably attained. We formerly were equally as eager and
equally as successful in compassing the seas for the same
ends ; **but latterly we are as a nation** abandoning **this
sphere of** enterprise and industry, and the question of **immediate interest is,** What **have we, as a nation, lost by so**
doing ?

And in reasoning upon **this subject, it is** important to
bear in mind that in foreign commerce the freights paid
on the things transported are as much exports or imports
as the merchandise which is exported or imported. Thus,
if 2,000 tons of coal of the value of $10,000 are sent in a
vessel of the United States to China, **and** the freight on
the same is $6,000, this freight is as much of an export of
the results of American industry as the coal itself ; and, if
paid and returned **to the United States** in the form of coin
or tea or silk, may, and under ordinary circumstances will,
add as much **proportionally to the** general wealth of the
country as the proceeds of the sale of the coal **upon** which
the freight was **earned.** On the other hand, if the coal is

transported in a foreign vessel, the freight earned **does**
not increase the capital or benefit the labor of the **United
States, but** of the country to which the vessel belongs.
In the case of importations the freights paid on the same
add to the cost and increase the volume or value of the
things imported ; and, if foreign vessels are employed, accrue exclusively to the benefit of the vessel and the country of its ownership, as much so as does **the** amount paid
for the import on which the freight was earned.   In other
words, if the tonnage of foreign vessels **engaged in the**
foreign import trade of the United States at present **earn**
annually for themselves some $45,000,000 to $50,000,000
(as they do), such earnings must be classed as foreign
imports, and, in default of an export of domestic com-
modities of corresponding value, must be settled for in
gold, or approved securities.   The value of such freight
imports is not generally known or considered in the discussion of **foreign** commercial relations, and, with a bal-
ance of trade largely **in favor of the United** States (as at
present, 1882) is not a disturbing element ; but if through
a diminished demand for our agricultural products, or
other causes, the value of our merchandise exports and
imports should be nearly or completely equalized, the im-
portance of this freight item of imports would be very
quickly made manifest.   On the contrary, if the imports
are transported in American vessels, the freights paid
accrue to American labor and capital ; and to the extent to
which that labor and capital has been profitably employed

If, however, by reason of natural conditions and circumstances, the exports and imports of the United States can be transported more cheaply and conveniently by the people and vessels of foreign countries than by our own people and vessels, it would be fighting against nature, and a waste of resources, to attempt to have it otherwise by paying subsidies (using this term in the sense of extraordinary payments), or, what is the same thing, hiring people to do what naturally it is not for their interest to do. But if, on the contrary, our inability to compete with foreigners in the carrying trade of the ocean is the result of our own bad management and stupidity, then the failure so to do is such a loss of opportunity and waste of resources as would, if general, result in complete national impoverishment and decrepitude.[1]

The amount annually paid for the transport of the exports and imports of the United States is variously esti-

---

[1] In "The North American Review" for June, 1880, Professor Sumner, in an article entitled, "Shall Americans own Ships?" contends that it is immaterial whether they do or not ; and that their sole matter of concern should be to secure freights at the lowest possible rates, and apply themselves exclusively to such industrial pursuits as pay best at home. As an abstract proposition, this position is undoubtedly logical : for, when men are free to decide as to what business they will engage in, they will always select that which seems to offer the best promise of profit ; and they require no outside help from legislation to instruct them on this point. But, in the case under consideration, the citizens of the United States are not free ; for the policy of their government does not permit them to profitably engage on equal terms with foreign ship-owners.

mated by different authorities, and admits of being only
approximately determined.   The most reliable estimates are
undoubtedly those which have been recently made by Mr.
Henry Hall of New York with the co-operation of Dr. E.
H. Walker, the former statistician of the New York Produce Exchange, and published in "The Atlantic Monthly"
for February, 1881.   By this writer the total payments for
freight money on American exports for the calendar year
1879 are fixed at $88,000,000 as a minimum, and about
$45,000,000 on imports, or an annual total of $133,000,000.
For the fiscal year ending June 30, 1880, Mr. Hall also
reports 18,000,000 of gross tons of the produce and manufactures of the United States as exported, and 3,900,000
tons of the produce and manufactures of foreign countries
as imported into the United States; the exports — grain,
provisions, cotton, petroleum, etc. — representing large
bulk in comparison with value, and the imports — tex-
tiles, drugs, manufactures of metals, etc. — large value in
proportion to bulk.

Of the above estimated aggregate of freights paid on
the exports and imports of the United States, probably
not more than one-fifth, or $26,000,000 as a maximum,
was carried under the American flag.   If the proportions
of the carrying trade of the United States alone, which
were controlled by us in 1860, namely, 65 per cent, had,
however, been simply maintained, without any increase,
then the present value of the business which we have
allowed to slip out of our hands in this department of our

domestic industry must be valued at $86,000,000 – $26,-000,000, or $60,000,000 per annum.

Adding to these estimates the loss of business consequent on the decline of ship-building and ship-repairing, and also the nearly total loss of the great business of ocean passenger and immigrant carriage, to be estimated for the year 1881 at not less than $20,000,000, and we have the sum of $100,000,000 as the smallest measure in money of the value of the business which is at present annually lost to the country in the department of industry under consideration, and also the minimum measure of benefit likely to accrue directly to our national industry if the lost business could be at once regained.

If we assume $100,000,000 as the loss which the business and national wealth of the country at present annually sustains by reason of the decay of our industries of ship-building, ship-repairing, and ship-using in foreign commerce, then this loss would be very nearly equivalent to all the capital invested in all the blast furnaces of the United States in 1880; to more than one-third of the value of the present annual products of all the iron and steel industries of the country; and to more than 50 per cent of the value of all the products of our cotton manufacture, as returned by the census of 1880.

But the direct losses occasioned by the decay of our ocean commercial marine are insignificant in comparison with the indirect losses due to the loss of trade from an inability to make exchanges promptly, regularly, and

cheaply, with foreign countries. No matter how well
stocked the **store** may be with good, cheap, and desirable
goods, if would-be customers find great inconveniences in
the way of getting to the store and in transporting to it
their products for barter or exchange, they will not come,
but trade elsewhere; more especially if they recognize that
some of the inconveniences in the **way of** their trading
have been purposely created, — that the road when injured
by natural causes has not **been** repaired, **and that** they are
obliged to journey **to the** store in wagons when they can
go elsewhere by cars with all modern improvements.

As illustrating, furthermore, the extent to which **the**
ocean carrying business is capable of development as a
national industry, and the important bearing which the
returns of such business may have upon the fiscal affairs
of a great commercial nation, attention is here asked to
the very remarkable results of an analysis of the international **carrying trade of Great Britain from** 1858 to
1876, inclusive, **as made by one of** the leading merchants
of Liverpool, — A. D. **McKay,** — and published **in** " The
London Economist" for December, 1877, with the inferen-
tial indorsement of that journal. Mr. McKay first shows,
from the official figures published by the British Board of
Trade, that the entire value of the imports into Great
Britain — merchandise, specie, and bullion — for the **nine-**
teen years from 1858 to 1876, was £5,986,000,000, and
that the value **of** all like exports for the same time was
£4,793,000,000; leaving an excess **of imports** over ex-

ports, or an apparent adverse balance of trade against the United Kingdom, for the period under consideration, of the immense sum of £1,193,000,000, or nearly $6,000,-000,000 ($5,965,000,000).

Mr. McKay then goes in to specify and explain in detail the several items of charges which should be deducted from the above returned value of imports; which are, *first and largest*, the freight carried by British vessels in bringing the imports into the country; second, marine insurance; third, port charges — wharfage, cartage, warehouse expenses, and the like; fourth, buyers' discount; fifth, foreign bill stamps; sixth, bankers' commissions; seventh, commission and brokerage. The sum thus shown to have been paid for freights and commercial charges on imports amounts to £518,400,000; and by this amount the officially returned value of the imports, considered in the light of a charge against the Kingdom, should be properly reduced.

Mr. McKay next gives in detail the several items that should be credited to the returned value of the exports from Great Britain for the nineteen years in question, and so added to their amount, which are as follows: first, freight money paid British ship-owners for carrying British exports; second, insurance; third, commissions; fourth, six months interest on goods sold for export; fifth, profits on goods exported. These several credits amount to £652,100,000; and by this sum he claims the returned value of exports is to be augmented. Now by these charges to imports, and credits to exports, aggregating £1,170,500,000 ($5,852,500,000), the apparent **adverse** trade balance against Great Britain from 1858 to 1876 **inclusive is** brought down to the comparatively small sum of £23,000,000 ; or, in other words, the exports and imports of the United Kingdom, for a considerable period of recent **years, are found to** very nearly balance **one** another as commercial transactions.

But the point **of** greatest interest and value brought out in this analysis — which, while perhaps open to criticism in some particulars, is undoubtedly substantially correct — is the fact that the earnings **of** that portion of the British merchant marine which is employed in carrying exports from and imports into the United Kingdom, and the commercial charges incident to the same, have amounted for a long period of years to an average of about $300,000,000 **per annum ; or a** sum sufficient to keep nearly balanced **the vast international account which** Great Britain maintains, greatly to the profit of **her labor and** capital, with all the world. **And** to this enormous return to Great Britain from the industry of carrying her own imports and exports must be added another amount, derived from her passenger transport on the ocean, and also from the earnings of that portion of her merchant tonnage employed by foreigners in an exclusively foreign carrying trade. How large a sum these earnings represent, cannot be definitely **stated ;** but they are beyond question sufficient to not only sink the £23,000,000 annual excess of

British imports over exports indicated by Mr. McKay's analysis above given, but also to always leave an immense balance of international trade in favor of Great Britain, subject to draft whenever circumstances may render its use expedient. And here also we find one, if not an all-sufficient, explanation of the circumstance that when a financial and industrial disturbance occurs at London, the great centre of British trade, its influence is felt in a greater or less degree throughout the whole world. And yet this business, in place of having touched its zenith of development, is probably only in its infancy.

Recent statistical inquiries, instituted in Europe, have led to the estimate that the value of the commerce of the globe for the year 1880 was about $14,405,000,000; an increase since 1850 of 240 per cent. Of this commerce Great Britain is believed to control 49 per cent ; while the toll which all nations pay to Great Britain for the carrying trade which she performs is represented "as equal to nearly 4 per cent of the exported value of the earth's products and manufactures."

In fact, with the exception of the railway interest, no branch of business has increased so rapidly within recent years as the ocean carrying trade ; and there is probably no branch of industry which, in proportion to the capital invested, has been more profitable. In comparison with factory investments, a statement has recently been published, that the industry employed in British shipping returns at present a gross equivalent of £300 for each man engaged in it ; while the corresponding **return for** each British factory operative is not in excess **of** £190 per annum.   The circumstance that **the** merchant **marine** of **the** world is at present expanding every year in increased ratios, is almost positive proof that its owners find **such** employment of their capital remunerative beyond the average ; while the further reported fact that the increase in the carrying trade of Great Britain alone, for 1881, was 7,764,000 tons in excess of 1879, is also sufficient proof that business for ships is not wanting.

CHAPTER III.

THE CAUSES OF THE DECADENCE OF THE AMERICAN MERCHANT MARINE.

HAVING inquired into and acquainted ourselves with the present condition of our ocean merchant-marine, and having traced the gradual changes which have taken place in our ship-building industry and foreign carrying trade within the last quarter of a century, we are now prepared to enter upon a discussion and analysis of the causes which have produced the existing most remarkable and at the same time nationally discreditable condition of this department of the nation's commerce and industry. How is it, that the United States, formerly a maritime power of the first class, has now no ships or steamers that can profitably compete for the carrying of even its own exports; not merely with the ships of our great commercial rival, England, but also with those of Italy, Sweden, Norway, Germany, Holland, Austria, and Portugal? And why is it that the commercial tonnage of nearly every nation annually increases, while the commercial tonnage of the United States, including coal-barges and canal-boats, annually declines, and exhibits no symptoms of recuperation? These are pertinent questions! They are questions which without solicitation ought to arrest the attention of every citizen of the United States who takes a particle of interest in the affairs of his country. They are questions which ought to be agitated and discussed, and discussed and agitated, in every schoolhouse, legislative assemblage, and newspaper in the country, until some remedial policy is agreed upon, and Congress is forced to adopt it. And, in entering upon the proposed field of inquiry, it is desirable to first clear away a mass of error and misapprehension which has accumulated in previous discussions by the efforts of those who have the faculty of darkening counsel by "words without knowledge."

What Agencies were not operative to occasion Decay.

The facts already presented fully demonstrate that the war was not the cause, and did not mark the commencement, of the decadence of American shipping; although the contrary is often and perhaps generally assumed by those who have undertaken to discuss this subject. The war simply hastened a decay which had already commenced; and, under the same influences and conditions as have otherwise prevailed, the same results which we now deplore would undoubtedly have been reached, even if no war had intervened. Neither can the paralysis with which the great branches of domestic industry under consideration have been smitten, and their even threatened extinction, be referred to such agencies as fluctuations of supply and demand, foreign wars, or financial revulsions at home or abroad ; for all these **influences** have operated in the past, but have produced **no** such results, **either in this** country or elsewhere, as those which have become a part of our recent commercial history. During the three years **last** past, the general prosperity of the United States, **measured** by the volume of business transacted and the **amount of** resulting profits, has been greater than ever **before**; and yet there has been not only no resuscitation **of the** American commercial marine, but rather a marked and further decline.

It was also a popular fancy a few years ago, **to** connect the decadence of American shipping to our then vicious, redundant, **and** irredeemable **currency**; **and at a commer-cial** convention held **in Boston, in** 1868, **there was** nothing in the speeches made that **commanded more** general assent and approval than the following statement **by a** delegate from Milwaukee: "Why," said he, "are your ships rotting at your wharves? It is because we are away from the rock bottom on which the nations of the earth transact business. When we get back to the right basis we shall again have free commercial intercourse with the world." And commenting on this proposition another delegate re-marked, "**Of course, with a redundant and** irredeemable currency we cannot compete **in the construction of ves-**sels with the people **of those** countries in which a specie standard prevails to **regulate prices and** give stability to values."

But our currency has now for three years been brought

back to a specie basis, and foreign nations in **this** respect
have no longer any advantage over us ; and yet there were
not half as many vessels or half as much tonnage **built in**
the specie year of 1880, as during the paper *régime* of
1868 ; and, if there were not more vessels rotting at our
wharves in 1882 than in 1868, it was because the rotting
process, in **default of** material to rot, cannot go on indefinitely.

But if the decadence **of** our shipping is not due to
domestic or foreign **wars, to** financial revulsions, or bad
money, to what **is** the deplorable result — which no **one**
denies has happened — to be attributed ? The answer **first**
is, to not one, but to several causes.

The Primary Cause of the Decay of our Merchant Marine.

The primary cause was what may be termed a natural
one, the result of the progress of the age and a higher
degree of civilization ; namely, the substitution of steam
in place of wind as **an agent** for ship-propulsion, and the
substitution of iron **in the place of wood** as a material for
ship-construction ; and for nations or individuals to have
attempted to permanently counteract the influence of these
substitutions by legislation or **any** specific **commercial**
policy, was as useless, as our own experience proves, as to
have sought to arrest the stars in their courses. So long
as wood was the article mainly used in the construction of
vessels, we had **an** advantage over **foreign nations** in the
cost of the material, in the skill which we had acquired in

working the same, and in the positive genius for the management of **wooden** sailing-ships which natural **faculty**
and more than two centuries of experience may be claimed
to have nationally engendered. When, however, the **steam-**
engine was substituted for the sail, and iron for wood, then
these advantages were in a great degree neutralized or
wholly swept away.

Steamships adapted to ocean navigation, and the successful application of iron to the construction of vessels
designed for ocean navigation, were accomplished facts in
Great Britain as early as 1837–38. As is generally the
case with all **new** inventions and discoveries, these startling innovations on an old established order of things
were **in the** outset regarded doubtfully, and, indeed, **did**
not command the full confidence of the commercial **pub-**
lic in both respects until a considerably later period.

The application of steam to ocean navigation was the
first to be accepted as an absolute necessity, and therefore as inevitable. The Americans waited until English
experience had proved the fact to their full satisfaction, and
then embraced the idea so eagerly, and turned it to practical account so rapidly, that the foreign steam-tonnage of
the United States, which really commenced to exist in
1848, nearly equalled in 1851 (as before shown) the **entire**
steam-tonnage of Great Britain of **longer growth, and**
continued to regularly and **largely** increase until 1856.
But during the period between 1848 **and** 1855, the commercial public had become pretty generally satisfied in

respect to certain other matters. They had been taught by further experience that iron in the construction of vessels was much more durable than wood, and that, whatever difference therefore there might be in the first cost, the iron vessel in the long-run is cheaper than the wooden one.[1] They had learned that iron vessels are more rigid than wooden vessels, and that the former are therefore better adapted to withstand the strain of heavy steammachinery, and also, that from lack of the necessary strength and rigidity the application of the most economical method of propulsion — namely, the screw — is impracticable in the case of wooden vessels of large capacity. They had also learned that iron ships are superior to wooden ships in buoyancy, and hence draw less water with a given tonnage, carry a greater weight of cargo, and have a greater stowage capacity. In short, they had come to know that for most practical purposes the iron ship was every way superior to the wooden ship; that the day for the latter had passed, and that the former was to be the vessel of the future. American ship-owners, merchants, and navigators, or at least the more enterprising of their number, were not more backward in learning and understanding the significance of these facts than their English competitors. In an article published in "The New-York Journal of Commerce," in the spring of 1857, nearly four years before the commencement of the Rebellion, Capt.

---

[1] However it may have been at the outset, the original cost of an iron vessel in England has for a long time been less than a wooden one.

John Codman, a practical, clear-headed New England sailor, fully understanding the then condition of affairs, and foreseeing the inevitable tendency of things in the future, wrote as follows : —

"In an article written some months since, it was assumed that steam was destined to be the great moving power for navigation, and that it would supplant almost entirely the use of sails. Experience is every day justifying this view, and still more it is becoming evident that steam will serve for the transportation of very much of the merchandise now carried by sailing-vessels. In fact, the time is not far distant when the latter class of ships will be required only for articles of great bulk and comparatively little value.

" The only question now is, Who are to be the gainers by this revolution in navigation ?

" Maintaining then as now that the screw must supersede the side-wheel for all purposes, and that iron screw-steamers are in all commercial respects preferable to wood steamers, the argument was advanced that England, being able to construct this class of vessels more economically than we can, must of necessity have the monopoly of building them. Her monopoly in this respect we cannot prevent, but it depends upon ourselves and our Government whether she shall share with us the monopoly of owning and sailing them.

" I have taken [continues Capt. Codman] a bold and it may be apparently an unpatriotic stand in assuming that the only way in which we can participate in ocean steam-navigation is in so changing our laws that we may buy her (English) steamers as she now buys our sailing-vessels, because she finds it for her interest so to do."

Had matters been allowed to take their natural course ; had Capt. Codman's wise advice — wise because in conformity with a large practical experience as a ship-owner

and ship-master — been followed in 1857; had Americans
been allowed to simply take the advantage of the world's
progress which was taken by their competitors, and had
not a subsequent restrictive commercial policy made foreign trade to American merchants almost impossible, — it
is certain, that, even in spite of the war, there would have
been no permanent material decline in the American shipping interest, and no such condition **of things** to bewail as
exists at present.   To assume to the contrary **is** to assume
that Americans would have made an exception of this one
department of their **domestic** industry, and have failed to
bring to it that sagacity and skill that before and since
have **characterized all their** other business operations.

But matters were not allowed to take their natural
course.   **The** means and appliances for the construction
of iron vessels did not then exist in the United States;
while Great **Britain,** commencing even as far back as 1837
(when John **Laird** constructed his first iron steamers of
any magnitude **for** steam navigation [1]), and with eighteen
years of experience, had become thoroughly equipped in
1855 for the prosecution of this great industry.   **The**
facilities for the construction of steam machinery **adapted**
to the most economical propulsion of ocean vessels, furthermore, were also inferior in the United States to those

---

[1] The first **iron steamer for ocean** navigation was really built as early as
1832, when the English **firm of Laird & Co.** constructed a small vessel of
fifty-five tons, which was **designed and** successfully used for the explora-
tion of the Niger.

existing in Great Britain ; and, by reason of statute provisions, citizens of the United States interested in ocean
commerce were absolutely prevented and **forbidden from**
availing themselves of the results of British skill **and su-**
periority in the construction of vessels when such **a re-**
course was the only policy which could have enabled them
at the time to hold their position **in** the ocean carrying
trade in competition with their foreign rivals.

Now, there is very little of sentimentality in respect to
business matters among the representatives of trade and
commerce, whatever may be their nationality.   They simply ask, "Who will serve us best and at **the** cheapest
rate ?"   And, **the** inability of the **ships of the** United
States to do **the** work which trade and commerce required
that they should do as well and cheaply **as** the ships **of**
other nations having been demonstrated by experience,
the decadence of American shipping commenced and was
inevitable from the very hour when this fact was first recognized, which was about the year 1856.

Here, then, we have the primary cause of the decay of
business of ship-building in the United States and of our
commercial **marine.**   Other causes — **to be hereafter**
noted — have since come in **and helped the decay, and are**
powerfully operative **to** prevent recovery ; but so **long as**
the conditions, which in the outset **were** the source of the
trouble, continue **to prevail, decay will** continue **to go** on,
and there can be no recovery.

Attention should here **be called to the** circumstance

that the relation of the United States to Great Britain in this matter of ship construction and employment has been no different, from the very outset of the new era in navigation, than that of all other maritime nations ; with the single exception, that, as the interest of the United States in the new conditions was greater than that of all these others combined, it was incumbent on the former to act with the greatest wisdom and discretion, and not allow prejudice and ancient conservatism to prevent the removal of obstacles which stood in the way of national growth and development. But none of these nations, with the possible exception of old Spain, acted as did the United States. Taking a practical, common-sense view of the situation, and setting sentiment aside, they concluded that it would be the height of folly to permit a great and profitable department of their industries to be impaired or destroyed, rather than allow certain improvements in the management of its details, because suggested and carried out by a foreign nation, to be purchased and adopted. And they therefore virtually said to their own people, "Go to, now! If England can build better and cheaper ships for ocean commerce than you can yourselves, and will furnish them to you on terms as favorable in every respect as is granted to her own citizens, and if your own private judgment and feeling of self-interest prompt you to buy and use such ships, the state will interpose no obstacles to your so doing. Furthermore, as between a business and the instrumentalities for doing business, we hold that the interests of the first are to be first considered: for, if the business fails, the instrumentalities employed in it, be they good or bad, will retain but little of value; whereas, on the other hand, if the business can be kept profitable there need be no apprehension as to a deficiency or imperfection of the instrumentalities."

And the merchants and capitalists of these maritime states, adopting the course which seemed best to them under the circumstances, went to England and supplied themselves with ships and steamers of the most approved patterns, and, sharing with the English the monopoly of owning and using the same, have always derived great profit therefrom. And the several states, furthermore, which permitted their citizens to act without restraint in accordance with their own best judgment in this matter, have never had any such results as the United States has experienced, but, on the contrary, have seen their commercial tonnage and carrying trade upon the high seas largely increase; and, if their shipping interests have since experienced any vicissitudes, they have not in any one instance been referred to influences even remotely connected with the liberal policy that was adopted.

On the other hand, the policy of the United States under the same circumstances has been very much as if, at the outset of the development of the railway system as an improved method of transporting goods and passengers, some one State of the Union — say Ohio, for example — had said, "We have no manufactories of locomotives or cars, or mills for rolling railway-bars, within our territory ; State pride, and a desire to be wholly independent, will not allow us to purchase these articles of Pennsylvania : therefore we will continue to use horses and wagons, which heretofore have answered our purposes of transportation, and not use railroads until we can manufacture all railroad equipments ourselves." People in other States would have been prompted to call the people of Ohio fools and stupids, and perhaps have prefixed to these terms of reproach and contempt certain irreverent and forcible expletives to add force to their expressions of sentiment ; and yet the boundary-line which separates the United States from Great Britain is just as much a matter of artificial ordination as that which separates Ohio from Pennsylvania. But, be this as it may, the result in the hypothetical case would have been exactly the same as is the result in the real case. Ohio would not have got her railroads, nor the wealth and development that would have flowed from their construction ; and the United States has not got the ships, or the wealth and business that have been attendant upon their possession and skilful employment in other countries.

The question which next naturally presents itself in the order of this inquiry and discussion is, Why is it that the people of the United States have not been permitted to enjoy the privileges accorded to other maritime nations, of adjusting their shipping interests to the spirit and wants of the age ? Why have they alone been debarred from using the best tools in an important department of commerce, when the using meant business retained, labor employed, and capital rewarded, and the non-using equally meant decay, paralysis, and impoverishment ? The answer is, Because of our so-called navigation laws. Let us, therefore, at this point consider the nature and influence of this famous code, which in a great degree has determined our commercial policy as a nation, and learn how it originated and why it has been perpetuated.

CHAPTER IV.

OUR NAVIGATION LAWS, AND HOW THEY ORIGINATED.

WHEN the convention that framed the Federal Constitution came together in 1787, there were two sectional
questions of importance that came before it, and two only,
— the question of slavery and the regulation of commerce.
The extreme Southern States wanted slavery and the
slave-trade legalized and protected. The South, as a
whole, also favored free trade. New England, on the
other hand, largely interested in shipping, a not insignificant proportion of which, either directly or indirectly, was
engaged in the slave-trade (her people, Massachusetts men
especially, importing molasses from the West Indies, dis-
tilling it into rum, using the rum to buy slaves on the
coast of Africa, and selling the slaves at the South), desired, through a system of navigation laws, to hold a
monopoly of the commerce of the new nation; while the
Middle States generally wanted neither slavery nor navigation laws. The sentiment of the country as a whole at
this period was averse to slavery; and the cultivation of
cotton not having then been introduced to any considerable extent into the Southern States, or made the source
of profit that it subsequently became through the inven-

tion of the cotton-gin, the anti-slavery feeling had developed itself much **more strongly in some parts of the South** than it had in New England.[1] So that, if New England

---

[1] " The sentiment was common to Virginia, at least among the intelligent and educated, that slavery was cruel and unjust. The delegates from Virginia and Maryland, hostile to navigation laws, were still more warmly opposed to the African slave-trade. Delaware by her constitution, and Virginia and Maryland by special laws, had prohibited the importation of slaves. North Carolina had shown a disposition to conform to the policy of her Northern sisters by an act which denounced the further introduction of slaves into the State as 'highly impolitic.'" (Hildreth, vol. iii., pp. 508–510.) Pennsylvania founded a society for the abolition of slavery in 1775, with Franklin for its first president, and Rush its first secretary. New York had a similar society in 1785, with Jay as its first president and Hamilton as his successor. On the other hand, as some illustration of the then current New England sentiment, attention is asked to the following extract from an oration by Mr. David Daggett (afterwards United States Senator and Chief-Justice of Connecticut) at New Haven, July 4, 1787, a month before the Federal Convention, then in session, took up the subject of slavery and the navigation laws. The orator, after speaking of the gratitude and generous reward the country owed to the officers and soldiers of the late army, and its immediate inability to discharge such obligations, continued,—

" If, however, there is not a sufficiency of property in the country, I would project a plan to acquire it. . . . Let us repeal all the laws against the African slave-trade, and undertake the truly benevolent and humane merchandise of importing negroes to Christianize them. This has been practised by individuals among us, and they have found it a lucrative branch of business. Let us, then, make a national matter of it. . . . We should have the sublime satisfaction of enriching ourselves, and at the same time rendering happy, thousands of those blacks, by instructing them in the ways of religion. . . . This would be no innovation. . . . This country permitted it for many years, among their other acts of justice ; but their refusing to pay sacred and solemn obligations is not so long standing."

had been as true to the great principles of liberty as her
people were always professing, it seems probable that,
aided by the Middle States, and in part by the South, she
might have brought about an arrangement under the Federal Constitution, at the time of its formation, for the
gradual but no very remote extinction of American slavery and an avoidance of the expenditure of blood and
treasure which has since been entailed by its continuance.
Selfishness and the love of the dollar, however, proved as
omnipotent then as they ever have, and the result was a
compromise of iniquity ; the power to regulate commerce
being inserted in the Constitution, together with and as a
consideration for the extension by New England votes of
the slave-trade until 1808 and the prohibition of export
duties.

A Curious Chapter of our National History.

This curious chapter in our national history, although
familiar to historical students, has been all but unknown
to the mass of the American people.   The evidence of its
truth is, however, complete.   The fourth section of the
Seventh Article of the Constitution of the United States,
as originally reported by the Committee of Detail, provided that " no tax or duty shall be laid by the Legislature on articles exported from any State, nor on the migration or importation of such persons as the several States
shall think proper to admit ; nor shall such migration or
importation be prohibited."   When the convention came

to the consideration of this section, they amended it by making the prohibition of the imposition of duties on exports general, or applicable to the Federal Government as well as to the States; although Mr. Madison tried to have the power to do so allowed to Congress when two-thirds of each House should vote its expediency. The question next occurred on the residue of the section, which Mr. Luther Martin, of Maryland, moved to amend so as to authorize Congress to lay a tax or prohibition at its discretion upon the importation of slaves. The provision as it stood in the report of the committee would, he said, give encouragement to the slave-trade; and he held it "inconsistent with the principles of the Revolution, and dishonorable to American character, to have such a feature in the Constitution." Messrs. Rutledge and Pinckney, the South Carolina delegates, and Mr. Baldwin of Georgia, warmly protested against Mr. Martin's proposition as an uncalled-for interference with the slave-trade. Mr. Ellsworth and Mr. Sherman, of Connecticut, were both for leaving the clause as reported. "Let every State," they said, "import what they please." Elbridge Gerry, of Massachusetts, "acquiesced, with some reserve," in the complying policy of the delegates of Connecticut; while his colleague, Rufus King, "made a measured resistance" merely on the grounds of State expediency. George Mason, of Virginia, expressed himself with great energy in opposition to the views of the delegates from Connecticut. "This infernal traffic," he said, "originated in the

avarice of British merchants;" and "he lamented that
some of our Eastern brethren had, from lust of gain, embarked in this nefarious traffic." In this state of things
Gouverneur Morris arose, and after adverting to the circumstance that the sixth section of the same Article of
the Constitution under consideration contained a provision
that no navigation laws should be enacted without the
consent of two-thirds of each branch of Congress, and
that this provision particularly concerned the interests of
the New England States, proposed that this section,
together with the fourth section (relating to the slave-
trade) and the fifth section (relating to the assessment of
a capitation tax on slaves), be referred to a special committee; remarking at the same time (see Rives's " Life
and Times of Madison," vol. ii., pp. 444, 450), "that these
things may form a bargain among the Northern and
Southern States."

The hint thus given was not thrown away. All these
matters were referred to a committee; and what this
committee did is thus told by Luther Martin, one of its
members, in a letter to the Speaker of the Maryland
House of Delegates : —

"I found the Eastern States, notwithstanding their aversion to
slavery, were very willing to indulge the Southern States at least with
a temporary liberty to prosecute the slave-trade, provided the Southern
States would in turn gratify them by laying no restriction on [the
enactment of] navigation acts; and after a little time the committee
agreed on a report by which the General Government was to be pro-

hibited from preventing the importation of slaves for a limited time, and the restrictive clause relative to navigation acts was to be omitted." (Elliott's "Debates," second edition, vol. i., p. 373.)

The limit of time for the extension of the slave-trade agreed to by the committee in making the bargain was 1800; but when the report came before the Convention, Mr. Pinckney of South Carolina moved to amend by substituting 1808 in lieu of 1800, as the term of the permitted traffic; and this motion was seconded by Mr. Gorham of Massachusetts. Mr. Madison and others earnestly opposed this amendment; "but the coalition that had taken place rendered all remonstrance vain, and Gen. Pinckney's motion was carried in the affirmative; all of the three New England States, with South Carolina, Georgia, Maryland, and North Carolina, voting for it, and Virginia, Pennsylvania, New Jersey, and Delaware voting against it." Four days later the residue of the report, recommending that the sixth section, which imposed restrictions against the passage of Congress of a navigation act be omitted, was taken up and earnestly debated, and opposed by George Mason, Gov. Randolph, and others, but as earnestly advocated by Pinckney and Butler of South Carolina, "who earnestly invoked a spirit of conciliation towards the Eastern States on account of the liberality they had shown to the wishes of the two southernmost States with regard to the importation of slaves;" and, finally, "the bargain that had been entered

into, oy which the legalization of the slave-trade for
twenty years on the one side was the price of the abandonment of restrictions on the passage by Congress of a
navigation act" on the other, received its final ratification.
(Rives's "Life and Times of Madison.")

The language of Hildreth in concluding his historical
account of this matter is also to the same effect, and is as
follows : "Thus by an understanding, or, as Gouverneur
Morris called it, 'a bargain,' between the commercial representatives of the Northern States and the delegates of
South Carolina and Georgia, and in spite of the opposition of Maryland and Virginia, the unrestricted power of
Congress to enact navigation laws was conceded to the
Northern merchants, and to the Carolina rice-planters, as
an equivalent, twenty years' continuance of the African
slave-trade." (Hildreth's "United States," vol. iii., p. 520.)

"This transaction," continues Mr. Rives, "undoubtedly
made a most disagreeable impression on the minds of
many members of the convention, and seemed at once to
convert the feeling of partial dissatisfaction, that had already been excited in certain quarters by one or two votes
of the convention, into a sentiment of incurable alienation
and disgust. Gov. Randolph, a few days after the first
part of the bargain had been ratified, and while the
latter part was pending, declared that 'there were features
so odious in the Constitution, as it now stands, that he
doubted whether he should be able to agree to it.' Col.
Mason, two days later, declared that 'he would sooner

chop off his right hand than put it to the Constitution as
it now stands.'" And the names of neither of these delegates appear on the roll of delegates to the national convention who subsequently signed the Constitution.

Ratification of the Contract.

When the Federal Congress assembled for the first time
under the Constitution, New England was not dilatory in
demanding the fulfilment of her part of this disreputable
compact; and in 1790 and 1792 the foundation of our
present navigation laws was laid, in acts levying tonnage
dues and impost taxes, which discriminated to such an
extent against foreign shipping as to practically give to
American ship-owners a nearly complete monopoly of all
American commerce. By the act of 1790, a tonnage tax
of thirty cents per ton was levied on all American vessels,
and fifty cents per ton on the vessels of powers not in
alliance with the United States. Duties in the ordinary
form on imports were also imposed, but a remission of ten
per cent of all such duties was provided in case the goods
were imported in American vessels.

These discriminating measures were provisionally repealed by the treaty of peace between the United States
and Great Britain in 1815: but, no disposition having
been subsequently manifested by Great Britain and other
foreign powers to enact reciprocal legislation, the repealing acts were never carried into effect; but on the contrary, in 1816, 1817, and 1820, Congress enacted a system

of navigation laws which were avowedly modelled on the
very statutes of Great Britain which the Americans, as
colonists, had found so oppressive that they constituted
one prime cause of their rebellion against the mother
country, the main features of difference between the two
systems being that wherever it was possible to make the
American laws more rigorous and arbitrary than the British model, the opportunity was not neglected.   And these
laws, without material change, hold their place to-day
upon our national statute-book.   International trade since
their enactment has come to be carried on by entirely different methods.   Ships are different, voyages are different,
crews are different, men's habits of thought and methods
of doing business are different : but the old, mean arbitrary laws which the last century devised to shackle commerce remain unchanged in the United States, alone of
all the nations ; and, what is most singular of all, it is
claimed to be the part of wisdom and the evidence of
patriotism to uphold and defend them.

As a further and essential part of the history of this
legislation, and as some extenuation of the illiberal policy
of the first Congress, it should be here stated that public
sentiment in the United States in respect to the policy of
the enactment of navigation laws, and of making them
harshly discriminative against the shipping of foreign
nations, experienced a marked change between the time
when the power to regulate commerce was made by the
convention a part of the Federal Constitution, and the

time when the enactment of discriminating tonnage dues and tariff taxes came up for consideration, in 1790 and 1792, in the Federal Congress. This was due mainly to the utter failure on the part of the American Government (confederative and constitutional) to induce Great Britain to recede in any degree from the extremely illiberal commercial policy which she had adopted towards her former colonies since the attainment of their independence. Previously they could trade freely with the other British possessions in America, and the West Indies, exchanging lumber, corn, fish, and other provisions, together with horses and cattle, for sugar, molasses, coffee, and rum; but immediately upon the conclusion of the war the people of the new nation were put on the same footing as other foreign countries, and under the operations of the British navigation laws were, in common with them, excluded from nearly all participation in an extensive and flourishing part of their former maritime commerce. And as illustrating the then temper of the times, and the illiberal spirit that then pervaded the counsels of nations, it may be mentioned, that this policy was persevered in by Great Britain, even after it was proved in repeated instances to work most injuriously to her own home interests, and to have occasioned great suffering upon her West-Indian colonies. Thus, between 1780 and 1787, no less than 15,000 slaves were known to have perished from starvation in the British West-Indies, by reason of inability, through the operation of the British navigation laws, to

obtain the requisite supplies of food from the North Americans at a period when the home-grown portion of their
substance had been destroyed by successive hurricanes.
William Pitt, however, was a man capable of rising above
the ordinary level of his times and political surroundings,
and, foreseeing the serious difficulties of the situation,
desired, as chancellor of the exchequer, immediately after
the close of the war, to deal liberally with the new nation ;
and accordingly, as early as 1783, introduced into Parliament a bill allowing comparatively free commerce between
the United States and the British colonies, — more especially with the West Indies.   But the measure, owing primarily to the resignation of the ministry, and to the
strong opposition of the British shipping interests, aided
by the efforts of the loyalists of the remaining British
North American colonies, was not only defeated, but in
1788 an act was passed absolutely forbidding the importation of any American produce into any British colony,
except in British bottoms.   And these restrictions on the
participation of the United States in British colonial trade
very singularly remained unrepealed until 1830, in which
year a British order in council was adopted authorizing
vessels of the United States to import into the British
possessions abroad any of their domestic produce, and to
export goods from the same to any foreign countries
whatever.

And, as some further evidence of the British jealousy
of the commercial competition of the United States during

the decade between 1783 and 1793, it may be mentioned that Lord Sheffield, who headed the opposition to **Mr. Pitt's** bill (above noticed), published in 1783 a book in which he advised the British Government not to interfere too extensively with the Barbary pirates, on the ground, that, through lack of any sufficient naval force on the part of the United States to restrain and punish, — but which force **Great** Britain was known to possess, — the operations of the corsairs would be confined mainly to the destruction of American commerce and of the little states of Italy, whereby British commerce would be benefited.[1]

Under such circumstances it was but natural that the

---

[1] The nature of the opinions respecting the commercial future of the United States, entertained after the termination of the war by not a few intelligent and influential Englishmen, is curiously illustrated by the following extract from the book of Lord Sheffield, above noticed, which, published originally about 1783 under the title, " Observations on the Commerce of the American States," appears to have attracted much attention in England, and to have passed through at least two editions. " The Americans," he says, " cannot protect themselves [from the Barbary States]; they cannot pretend to a navy. In war New England may have privateers, but they will be few indeed if we do not give up the Navigation Act. The best informed say not less than three-fourths of the crews of the American privateers during the late war were Europeans. It has been shown that America has not many sailors, and they are not likely to increase if we are prudent; and when Irishmen learn to employ themselves better than in fighting the battles of the Americans, by sea as well as by land, the character of the latter will not in general be very martial their condition, state, circumstances, intents, must prevent. It is remarkable how few good harbors there are for large ships-of-war in the American **States south of** Cape Cod; at least, we have found none **except at** Rhode Island : **and,** if a navy could be afforded, there would be

representatives of the nation came together in **Congress in**
1791–92 with very different sentiments in respect **to policy**
of navigation laws from those entertained by the members
of the Federal Convention in 1787.　It was felt by **the for-**
mer, and by the whole nation, that the legislation of Great
Britain — especially that part of it which broke up the
then important trade of the United States with the British West Indies — was designedly hostile legislation,
which could only **be** properly met, and its continuance
prevented, by retaliatory legislation.　And Congress in
1790–92 accordingly did retaliate; and a quarter **of a**
century later (1816–1820), **after** another war, when **Great**

---

as much difficulty in agreeing that so essential an establishment should be at
Rhode Island as there would be in removing the Dutch Admiralty from
Amsterdam.　To the southward of the Bay of Fundy there is not flow of
tide sufficient to enable the Americans to have a dry-dock for ships of the
line.　The want of durability in their timber would alone make a navy most
expensive to them.　A country which has such opportunity of farming cannot
be supposed to support many seamen.　There is not a **possibility of** her
maintaining a navy.　That country, concerning which writers of lively imagi-
nations have lately said so much, is weakness itself.　Exclusive of its poverty
and want of resources, having lost all credit, its independent government,
discordant interests, and the great improbability of acting again together,
the circumstance alone of such a vast country, with a third less of people
than that small spot in Europe inhabited by the Dutch, are incompatible
with strength.　Her population is not likely to increase as it has done, at
least on her coast.　On the contrary, the present inhabitants **are** likely to
fall back on the interior country to get better land, and avoid taxes; and
that they may in some future ages become numerous as a country of farmers,
without markets, can be expected; but the settlers beyond the Alleghany
Mountains cannot become commercial."

Britain refused to accept the offer on the part of the United States of a more liberal reciprocal commercial policy, it enacted navigation laws even more stringent than any which had before found a place upon our statute-books.

To further complete this record, it should be also here noted, that, in connection with the restriction of commerce by the enactment of navigation laws in the first Congress, the first selfish and sectional antagonism of the States, in respect to the adjustment of duties on foreign imports, also occurred. Thus "the South" (we quote from Professor Sumner's "History of Protection in the United States") "wanted a protective duty on hemp, claiming that rice and indigo were unprofitable. Pennsylvania opposed any tax on hemp as a raw material of cordage, but wanted a tax on that. New England opposed the tax on cordage as a raw material of ships, but wanted protection on the latter." The most strenuous contention was, however, in respect to rum and molasses. "The South, except Georgia, wanted a high tariff on rum for revenue. The Middle States wanted it in the interests of temperance; the Eastern States, for protection to their rum-distilleries. Georgia opposed this tax because she used a great deal of rum, and bought it in the West Indies with her lumber. The Southern and Middle States wanted a tax also on molasses, but this the Eastern States vigorously opposed. Molasses was the raw material of rum." It was bought with salt fish, lumber, and staves sent to

the West Indies, distilled into rum in New England, which
was sent as export to Africa to buy slaves, and these in
turn were sold to the South.   And now, after having
bartered **their souls by** extending the horrors of the
slave-trade **for** twenty long years **in** consideration of a
monopoly of shipping, was New England to permit the
most profitable element of that monopoly to be at once
taken away from them ?   Not if their representatives
could prevent it !   We are accustomed to look back upon
the representatives that sat in the first Congress, especially those sent from New England, as men infinitely
removed from base and sordid motives, whose like it is
never to be vouchsafed to us to see again in public office.
But, when one comes to look over the debates that took
place in the first Congress on the rum and molasses ques-
tion, he cannot help fancying that he is in the Federal
House of Representatives **at** the present **day,** and that a
debate on the **tariff** is in progress.

   The duty **which** it was proposed **to** assess on molasses
was six cents a gallon, — a fourth of a cent less than
molasses pays under the existing tariff (1882) ; and the
delegation from Massachusetts, it is recorded, "occupied
the time of the House for **several** days with vehement
remonstrances against it."   One member, Mr. Thurber,
went so far as to intimate that the people of his State
"will hardly bear a tax which they cannot but look upon
as odious **and** oppressive."   **Mr.** Fisher Ames, in an ex-
travagant speech on the woeful effects likely to follow the

enactment of the proposed duty on molasses, used the following language : "Mothers will **tell** their children, when they solicit their daily and accustomed nutriment, that the new law forbids them the use of it ; and they will grow up in detestation of the hand which proscribes their innocent **food** and the occupation **of their** fathers." And yet all **the** while none knew better **than** Fisher Ames that **the** mothers likely to be most **distressed** were the owners of distilleries, and that the occupation of the fathers that the children were to be debarred from following was sending this rum to Africa to be used **to buy** slaves. **New** England selfishness again triumphed. The proposed duty on molasses **was** reduced from six cents to **two and a half** cents a gallon, **and** rum **was** assessed at ten cents **per** proof gallon, while all other **spirits were to pay but** eight cents.

Such, then, is a brief history of the inception and **growth** of our present navigation laws. Conceived in sin **and** brought forth in iniquity, they seemed to have entailed **a curse** (not yet fully worked out, but in the **process of completion),** general for the **whole country, but more** especially **on that** section whose **fathers sold their honor** to accomplish **the** result, and **who thereby merited exe-**cration for having entailed, for **eighteen long** years, the horrors of the African slave-trade. **And when one** journeys through New England, and sees how thick **are the** graves of her sons, slain in **a war which** slavery originated, **the** question might suggest **itself : Would these** graves

exist, had the ancestors of those who fill them not con-
sented to strengthen and perpetuate domestic slavery as
a consideration for the privilege of doing another wrong ;
namely, that of restricting their fellow-citizens from freely
exchanging the products of their labor ?

CHAPTER V.

THE PROVISIONS OF OUR NAVIGATION LAWS.

HAVING traced the inception and growth of the navigation laws of the United States, let us next inquire into their provisions. They may be, in the main, stated and illustrated as follows : —

1. No American citizen is allowed to import a foreign-built vessel, in the sense of purchasing, acquiring a registry or title to, or of using her as his own property ; the only other absolute prohibitions of imports, on the part of the United States, being in respect to counterfeit money and obscene publications or objects. — *Revised Statutes of the United States*, sect. 4,132.

Furthermore, while we are the only people in the world who are forbidden to purchase foreign-built vessels, we freely permit all the world to enter our ports with vessels purchased in any market. Precluded, therefore, by the first provisions of our navigation laws, from engaging on equal terms in the carrying trade with foreigners, we wonder and complain that the carrying trade of even our own products has passed from our control.

2. An American vessel ceases to be such if owned in the smallest degree by any person *naturalized* in the

United States who may, after acquiring such ownership, reside "for more than one year in the country in which he originated, or more than two years in any foreign country, unless such person be a consul or other public agent of the United States." — *United States Revised Statutes*, sect. 4,134.

3. If a native-born American citizen, for health, pleasure, or any other purpose, except as a consul of the United States or as a partner or agent in an exclusively American mercantile house, decides to reside (" usually ") in some foreign country, any American vessel of which he may be, in all or any part, owner, at once loses its register, and ceases to be entitled to the protection of the flag of the United States, even though the vessel may have been of American construction, and have regularly paid taxes in the United States, and the owner himself has no thought of finally relinquishing his American citizenship. — *United States Revised Statutes*, sect. 4,133.

To illustrate this provision of our navigation laws, let us suppose Capt. John Smith, not a naturalized citizen, but a native American, is an owner, in all or part, of an American vessel. He becomes afflicted with a disease of the lungs, and, for his health, goes to live in the South of France, on account of the balmy atmosphere that prevails there. The moment that Capt. John thus, under the law, begins to "usually reside" in a foreign country, his vessel is liable to lose its register and the protection of the flag of his country.

4. Every citizen of the United States obtaining a register for an American vessel must make oath "that there is no subject or citizen of any foreign power or state directly or indirectly, by way of trust or confidence, or otherwise, interested in such vessel or in the profits thereof." — *United States Revised Statutes*, sect. 4,142.

We invite foreign capital to come to us, and help build our railroads, work our mines, insure our property, and even buy and carry our government bonds as investments; but if a single dollar of such capital is used to build an American ship, and thereby represents an ownership to any extent of the value received, we declare the ship to be thereby so tainted as to be unworthy of the benefit of American laws.

5. A foreigner may superintend an American factory, run an American railroad, be president of an American college, or hold a commission in the American army, but he cannot command or be an officer of a registered American vessel. — *United States Revised Statutes*, sect. 4,131.

Notwithstanding this express provision of law, it is an indisputable fact that there is hardly an American vessel engaged in foreign trade that has not one or more foreigners employed as officers; and instances, it is said, are not rare, of American vessels which have no citizens of the United States on board except the master.

If Capt. John Smith, being a foreigner, took command of an American vessel, and falsely swore that he was an American citizen, he would "forfeit and pay the sum of one thousand dollars." **If one** of the owners should take such oath, Capt. Smith **not** being in the district, the vessel would be subject to forfeiture; but no such case of forfeiture has ever occurred. She would, however, not be subject to forfeiture " **if** Capt. Smith **had** been appointed **the lowest** officer on **the** vessel." To be sure, the law requires that " officers of **vessels of the** United States shall in all cases **be citizens of the** United States;" but there is no penalty whatever imposed **on the vessel** if they are not.

Many American citizens, on the other hand, undoubtedly own vessels under **foreign** flags. Some **of them** transferred their vessels to English colors during the **war,** to escape capture by Confederate war vessels; but there **are** many who adopt this expedient to obtain cheap ships. They engage **a** trustworthy English clerk, for instance, **and** buy the vessel in his name, holding a mortgage for **her full value as security.**

Some years ago **the American consul-general** to China — Mr. Seward — **in a report to the** State Department stated, as within his personal experience from 1862 to 1875, " that the rigid enforcement **of** this law would often have forced the owners or agents of those vessels **engaged in** that part of the world to lay up their ships or transfer **them to** other flags."

6. **No** foreign-built vessel, or vessel in any part owned by a subject of **a** foreign power, can enter a port of the **United States, and then go to** another domestic port with

any new cargo or with any part of her original cargo that
has been once unladen, without having previously voyaged
to and touched at some other port of some foreign country, under penalty of confiscation. By a comparatively
recent construction of the law, all direct traffic by sea
between the Atlantic and Pacific ports of the United
States *via* Cape Horn or the Cape of Good Hope, or
across the Isthmus of Panama, is held to be of the nature
of a coasting trade or voyage in which foreign vessels
cannot participate. — *United States Revised Statutes*, sect.
4,347.

In view of the fact that there has been no attempt in
recent times, on the part of the English, French, or Dutch
governments, to interfere with the transport of merchandise by American ships by the common highway of the
ocean, between the home ports of these countries and
their colonial possessions, this construction of law, not
contemplated at the period of its enactment, was regarded
by Europe as a bit of very sharp and mean practice on the
part of the United States, as it undoubtedly was.

7. An American vessel once sold or transferred to a
foreigner can never be bought back again and become
American property, not even if the transfer has been the
result of capture and condemnation by a foreign power in
time of war. — *United States Revised Statutes*, sect. 4,165.

8. A vessel under thirty tons cannot be used to import
any thing at any seaboard port. — *United States Revised
Statutes*, sect. 3,095.

9. Goods, wares, and merchandise, the produce of countries east of the Cape of Good Hope, when imported from countries west of the Cape of Good Hope, are subject to a duty of ten per cent in addition to the duties imposed on such articles when imported *directly*.[1] This law is interpreted so stringently that old second-hand gunny-bags, nearly worn out, do not lose their distinctiveness to an extent sufficient to exempt them from additional duties if they finally come to the United States, in the process of using, from a place west of the Cape of Good Hope. A few years ago a vessel from China, destined to Montreal, Canada, was sent, on arriving, to New York without breaking bulk. It was held that the voyage ceased in Canada, and that the new voyage to New York subjected the cargo to an additional ten per cent. By the original navigation laws (Act of 1790) it was provided that the tariff on all articles imported in American vessels shall be less than if imported in foreign vessels. On "Hyson" tea the duty in American vessels was twenty cents per pound, in foreign vessels forty-five cents. The present discriminating duties on products of countries east of the Cape of Good Hope, imported indirectly, are a remnant and legacy of these old restrictions. — *United States Revised Statutes*, sect. 2,501.

10. If a vessel of the United States becomes damaged on a foreign voyage, and is repaired in a foreign port, her

[1] This provision of law, after an experience of over ninety years, the present Congress (1882) has repealed after Jan. 1, 1883.

owner or master must make entry of such repairs **at a** custom-house of the United States, as an import, and pay a duty on the same equal to one-half the cost of the foreign work or material, or fifty per cent *ad valorem;* and this law extends so far as to include boats that may be obtained at sea from a passing foreign vessel in order to assure the safety of the crew or passengers of the American vessel. — *United States Revised Statutes,* sect. 3,114.

To the credit of former days it should be said that this provision of law was not a part of the original navigation laws of the United States, but was incorporated into them by special statute passed July 18, 1866, entitled "An Act to prevent Smuggling and for other purposes." Under the Treasury regulations it is held that, although **no part of** the proper equipment of a vessel arriving in the United States from a foreign country is liable to duty, such equipment, if considered by the United States revenue officers as redundant, is liable to the payment of duty as a foreign import, although there may be no intent of landing, disposing of, or using such extra equipment, except in connection with the vessel. Thus, for example, when two sets of chains were found on **board** of a foreign vessel, and one set was held to be all that was necessary, the other set was made chargeable with duty. In another case, where anchors and chains were bonded on importation, and at the same time entered for exportation, and placed on board the vessel as a part of her equipment, it was held by the Treasury that the legal duties should be collected on the same.

11. Foreign vessels losing rudder, sternpost, or breaking shaft, and arriving in the United States in distress, cannot import others to replace these articles here without payment of the duty on the same. In one case of actual occurrence, a foreign line of steamers left — during a trip interval — their mooring-chains, of foreign manufacture, on an American wharf. Some over-vigilant revenue-officer reported the occurrence to the Treasury Department, and it was decided, that, as the chains were landed, the legal duties should be collected from them as an importation. A foreign vessel cannot even land copper sheathing for the sole purpose of being re-coppered by American workmen, without paying duties on the old copper stripped off, and the new copper put on, as separate and distinct imports. During the year 1871 the owner of a Dutch vessel entered at Boston, ignorant of the peculiar features of the tariff of the United States in respect to the ocean carrying trade, put on board, at the foreign port of clearance, a quantity of sheet-copper sufficient to sheath the bottom of his vessel, it being intended to have the work done in the United States upon her arrival, in order to save time, and put the vessel in good order for her return voyage. The agent, advised of this arrangement, referred the matter to the officials of the Boston custom-house for instructions, only to learn that the new sheathing-metal could not be used in the United States as proposed, without paying a duty of forty-five per cent, while the copper taken off the ship's bottom must also pay a duty of four

cents per pound as an importation of old copper. The
agent signified his willingness to pay the latter, and sell
the old metal for what it would bring, but requested to be
allowed to land the new copper in bond for re-exportation.
as it would be carried out by the same vessel that brought
it in. He was informed, however, that the bond for exportation required for its cancellation a certificate of the
landing of the bonded goods in the foreign port for which
its export was declared, which could not be obtained if it
was entered at the port of destination upon, and not in,
the ship carrying it. The consequence was, that when
the ship discharged her cargo at Boston, she sailed for
Halifax, N.S., carrying her sheathing-copper with her,
and after having been there coppered by the shipwrights
of the British Provinces returned in ballast to Boston for
her return cargo, — all this costly proceeding being cheaper
than the payment of forty-five per cent duty for the privilege of employing American workmen to take off the old
sheathing and put on the new.

12. If a citizen of the United States buys a vessel of
foreign build which has been wrecked on our coast, takes
her into port, repairs, and renders her again serviceable
and seaworthy, he cannot make her American property,
unless it is proved to the satisfaction of the Treasury
Department, that the repairs put upon such vessel are
equal to three-fourths of the cost of the vessel when so
repaired. — *United States Revised Statutes*, sect. 4,136.

The following is an illustration of the working of this

statute : In 1871 a citizen of Baltimore purchased **a foreign**-
built vessel wrecked on the American coast, and abandoned
to the underwriters, and, by spending a large sum in **recon**-
struction, rendered her again seaworthy.   He then, being
desirous of employing his capital embodied in this instrumentality of trade in the most profitable manner, and
assuming that the reconstructed wreck was his lawful
property, arranged for an outward cargo, under the flag
of the United States.   But when the vessel was ready to
sail, registry was refused by the customs officials, on the
ground that the vessel was of foreign construction, — the
sum of the repairs put on the wreck being a little less
than three-fourths of the original cost of the vessel ; or,
in other words, the substance of this decision, which was
correct in law, was, that while the citizen, under the laws
of the United States, might lawfully buy and acquire title
to a wreck, and use it for any purpose other than navigation, — as, for example, as a dock, a house, or a coal-bin,
— **he** could **not** acquire title to it and make it American
property, lawful to use as a vessel, even after he had paid
duties on its old materials as imports, unless he could
show that he had expended upon the abandoned construction, for the purpose of restoring it to its original quality
for service, a sum nearly equivalent to the cost of building
an entirely new vessel.   The owner by law, most merci-
fully, in such cases is not, however, deprived of the privilege of selling the property to a foreigner.

13. Every vessel belonging to the mercantile marine

of the United States engaged in foreign trade — vessels employed in the fisheries excepted — must pay annually into the Federal Treasury a tonnage-tax at the rate of thirty cents per ton. — *United States Revised Statutes*, sect. 4,219.

At the commencement of the war there were no tonnage taxes ; but by the Act of July, 1862, a tonnage-tax of ten cents per ton was imposed, which was afterwards increased to thirty cents, the present rate. Although there was nothing specific in the recent enactments to warrant it, and American shipping engaged in foreign trade was in such a condition as to demand the kindliest consideration from Government, the Treasury officials, interpreting the statute according to the invariable rule for the benefit of the Government and to the disadvantage of the citizen, were in the habit, up to 1867, of collecting this tax at every entry of a vessel from a foreign port ; but by the Act of March, 1867, tonnage taxes can now be levied but once a year. On a ship of one thousand tons the present tax, amounting to three hundred dollars per annum, represents the profits or interest — reckoned at six per cent — on an invested capital of five thousand dollars, and on a ship of two thousand tons of ten thousand dollars. Mr. F. A. Pike of Maine, in a speech in the United States House of Representatives, May, 1868, stated that this tax was equivalent, in many instances, to three per cent on the market valuation of an inferior class of American vessels, employed only in the summer months, and largely owned by his constituents.

Vessels belonging to foreign states, between whom and the United States ordinary commercial relations are established, pay the same tonnage-taxes as American vessels. But if any person not a citizen of the United States becomes an owner, to the extent of the merest fraction, in a ship of American build, then such ship is not entitled to the privileges accorded to ships owned wholly by foreigners, but must pay on entering a port of the United States a tonnage-tax of sixty cents, or double rate, and such vessel at once ceases to be entitled to registry or enrolment as a vessel of the United States. Here, then, we have piled up, as it were, on the top of all other provisions, another direct, odious, and stupid discrimination against the employment of foreign capital, provided it should so incline, for the developing of the American shipping interest and the employment of labor even in our own dockyards and harbors. Supposing a similar law to be proposed, discriminating in like manner against the investment of foreign capital in American railroads, mines, factories, and mercantile enterprises generally, does any one doubt that the proponent would be at once hooted into contempt? And yet the hypothetical law is no more absurd than the law that actually exists upon the statute-book.

Practically the law is a dead letter. In the case of ordinary vessels rigid inquiry as to ownership is rarely or never instituted, and the oath required is regarded and taken as a mere form. In case of incorporated American ocean navigation companies (if there are any such) the president of the company has only to swear to the ownership of any vessel by the company, and the Federal officials will not care if the ownership of one or a majority of the shares of the corporation vest in citizens of foreign nationalities ; the provision of the statute, as with a view of making the law of non-effect, being, that, in this swearing to ownership by a company, it shall not be necessary to designate the names of the persons comprising such company. The result of this is, that any foreigner can purchase shares in any American navigation company, and not a vessel of their fleet will thereby lose American registration and American protection ; but if a foreigner became the owner of the smallest fraction of a hundred-ton steamboat, plying between Key West and Havana, the registration of such vessel would be immediately vitiated.

If a Sunday-school or a picnic party, out on an excursion, happen to come into an American port on a foreign (Canadian) vessel (as was recently the case on one of our upper lakes), for mere temporary and pleasure purposes, the vessel is liable to a tonnage-tax ; and a libel against the vessel, instituted by an over-zealous official for its payment, was decided by the Treasury Department (August, 1876) to be a proceeding which the Government must enforce.

14. By the Act of June 6, 1872, all materials necessary for the construction of vessels built in the United States

for the purpose of foreign trade may be imported and used free of duty. But no American vessel receiving the benefit of this act can engage in the American coasting trade for more than two months in any one year without payment of the duties which have been remitted.

15. The several ports of the United States are classified by districts; and in each district one port is designated by statute as a "port of entry," and others as "ports of delivery." All vessels, on arriving from a foreign country in any district, must first report at the established port of entry, and there conform to the details of the custom-house service; after which the vessel, if American, can proceed, if desired, to any port of delivery in the district for the purpose of unloading. But if the vessel be foreign, it can only discharge at the port of entry, even though its cargo be imported exclusively for the use of American citizens at a port of delivery. A ship, therefore, may pass almost within hail of the point of destination of its cargo, and yet be compelled to unload many miles away, thus necessitating re-shipping and repeated handling, at much additional expense. Thus, the customs district of Boston and Charlestown comprises only one port of entry, — Boston, — while Cambridge, Medford, Hingham, Cohasset, etc., are all ports of delivery only. If a foreign vessel arrives from abroad with a cargo of hemp for Hingham, instead of proceeding direct to the wharf in that port, she must first sail right by, enter herself and cargo in Boston, and then unlade at a Boston

wharf, when the goods may be re-shipped by packet or railroad for Hingham. Again : if a foreign vessel is loaded with a cargo for Saybrook, a port of delivery at the mouth of the Connecticut River, she must pass directly by her destination, and proceed forty miles up the river — often with difficulty navigable — to Middletown, the port of entry for the district, and there discharge, and provide for the reconveyance of her cargo by some other method of transportation to the place where it is wanted.

The following will also illustrate in some degree the manner in which the navigation laws of the United States have been executed : —

All vessels of the United States engaged in the coasting trade are required to be enrolled and licensed; and vessels engaging in trade and transportation without previously procuring such enrolment or license are liable to seizure and heavy penalties. On the east bank of the Hudson, in the city of Troy, State of New York, there are extensive iron-works, the coal and ore supplies for which are largely transported over the Erie and Champlain Canals. Boats coming down these canals loaded with such supplies are locked into the Hudson at West Troy, a point on the west bank nearly opposite to the furnaces ; then, after crossing the river, delivering their freight, and recrossing, re-enter the canal, and return on their route for another similar cargo. Some years ago the officials of the United States Treasury Department decided that under our navigation laws this temporary entry of boats from the canals into the Hudson for the purpose of delivering cargo, and their subsequent return into the canal, constituted a coasting voyage, for the engaging in which it was obligatory on the owners of the canal-boats to have previously taken out a license. Of course the owners, not anticipating any such official interpretation of the law, had not provided themselves with licenses; but this nevertheless did not prevent a large number of boats from being seized and libelled for violation of the navigation laws, from which they were only released after expensive and annoying litigation and the payment of considerable sums in the way of costs or penalties.

Take another illustration of more recent date. It has of late years been customary for merchants and shippers on our northern lakes to buy and use for transporting grain large barges or hulks built in Canada; and as such constructions are not capable of moving or navigating except as they are towed, and are not provided with the usual appurtenances for navigation, they have not been regarded as subject to the provisions of our navigation laws relative to foreign vessels. During the summer of 1880, however, the collector of the port of Erie, Penn., on Lake Erie, called the attention of the Treasury Department to the circumstance that a certain barge, "The William H. Vosburg," had been guilty of the heinous offence of hoisting a sail on its apology for a mast, — whether for the sake of avoiding a dangerous rock or a lee shore was not stated, — and asked for instructions. The Department promptly replied, "that the only condition upon which that barge could continue to navigate those waters was to hoist her sails temporarily ; any attempt to keep her canvas up beyond that would get her into trouble. Being Canadian built, she could not be enrolled ; and, by consequence, the permanent use of sail upon her would entail forfeiture of cargoes and the payment of double tonnage-tax at every port of arrival." The official correspondence does not inform us what the result was ; but it is safe to presume the little barge had to take down her little sail, as otherwise she would have been simply taxed out of existence, in accordance with the statutes in such cases made and provided.

In August, 1875, the Canadian yacht "Oriole," of less than fifty tons burden, owned in Toronto, but belonging to the International Yacht Club, and also to the Yacht Club of Detroit, arrived in Chicago from Toronto with a pleasure-party of seven gentlemen, for the purpose of participating, on invitation of the Chicago Yacht Club, in a regatta at the latter port, having previously made a tour of the lakes, stopping at various points of interest, and taking on board on several occasions pleasure-parties of ladies and gentlemen, who were entertained in part by transportation from port to port. On arrival at Chicago "The Oriole" was complained of to the Treasury Department as having violated the navigation laws of the United States, which forbid foreign vessels from participating in the coasting trade and from conveying passengers from one American port to another; and proceedings looking to seizure and confiscation were contemplated. This **penalty** the Secretary of the Treasury graciously remitted, inasmuch as there was evidently no intent on the part of the **owners of " The Oriole " to violate the** law; but owing **to the absence of** proper **papers** showing the **nationality and** occupation of the yacht, although these were well known, the privilege of exemption from tonnage-taxes accorded by law to foreign pleasure-yachts was not granted. The Chicago Yacht Club therefore paid on account of their guests, into the treasury of the United States, the sum of fifteen dollars, which doubtless helped to liquidate the public debt; while the owners of " The Oriole," not knowing what other legal difficulties they might encounter from a prolonged sojourn, slipped out of port in the early morning, and returned home as soon as practicable.

We are accustomed, as we read of **the** sumptuary laws and arbitrary restrictions on commercial and personal freedom in years long past, to congratulate ourselves, as it were involuntarily, that we live on a higher and different plane, and that among nations calling themselves civilized and enlightened, such things are no longer possible. It would be difficult, however, to find in any record of past experience more absurdities and iniquities than are embodied in **the** so-called navigation laws of the United States at present existing, and in the details of their administration during the last quarter of a century. And yet it was in respect to these same laws that a convention of one of the great political parties, held in Maine in August, 1877, unanimously resolved that, " enacted in the infancy of the Republic, they have proved their wisdom by long and varied experience. They embody the matured judgment of three generations of commercial men. Any radical change in these laws would be detrimental to the highest interests of American commerce, and a damaging blow to the national independence of the country."

In answer to the questions which must naturally here suggest themselves to every thoughtful mind, How is it that such a code of laws — which no other civilized coun' try would permit to remain upon their statute-books — can at this period of the nineteenth century be maintained and defended in the United States ? and how happened it that a convention of presumably more than average intelligence could make public declaration of such nonsense and untruth as was embodied in the resolutions of the Maine convention above quoted ? — it may be said that upon no one public matter have the American people, until within a very recent period, been so little acquainted as in respect to our commercial laws and regulations. Scattered through statute enactments for over ninety years, and with court and treasury interpretations for the same period forming a part of the law and all of its administration, though not embodied in the statute, it has not been an easy matter for even those engaged in the

business of law and law-making to know what the navigation laws actually were ; and it is exceedingly doubtful
whether in the convention referred to there was one single
man that had any clear and definite knowledge of how
these laws originated, what they embody, and what is the
sphere of their influence.

And to-day, notwithstanding recent discussions of their
nature, it is doubtful whether, out of the three hundred
and seventy-eight members of Congress, as many as fifty
can at once define the difference between a vessel "enrolled" and a vessel "registered ;" or if any of the officials
of the customs service or Treasury Department can at
once, and correctly, tell in detail how to transfer the
license of a merchant-ship or pleasure-yacht from one
collection district of the United States to another.[1]   And
it is further curious to note that not a single writer or
speaker of note, who, within recent years, has undertaken
to advocate the navigation laws of the United States, or
oppose their repeal or essential modification, — possibly
from lack of knowledge, or fear lest a full exposition would
of itself defeat and neutralize his argument, — has ever
ventured to tell his readers or hearers what the code really
embraces or provides for in detail.

---

[1] It required some of the best legal talent in the city of New York, a few
years since, to effect this result in the case of a pleasure-yacht ; and the
owner of the yacht writes, that although he has done his best, and incurred
considerable expense and no end of trouble, to find out the law and comply
with it, he is in daily expectation of a visit from the revenue officials of the
United States, and a notification of a fine for some violation of the statutes.

CHAPTER VI.

HOW AND WHY GREAT BRITAIN REPEALED HER NAVIGA-TION LAWS, AND THE RESULTS OF REPEAL.

AT the period when the navigation laws of the United States were mainly enacted — 1789–1820 — all other maritime nations had similar codes. But since then all maritime nations, except the United States, have either greatly modified the old-time restrictions which they once imposed on the building and use of vessels, or abolished them altogether, — Chinese and Japanese commercial exclusiveness having even yielded to the liberal spirit of the age. In this reform work Great Britain took the lead at the very time (1849) when the competition of the United States with that nation for the carrying trade of the world upon the high seas was most severe, and when whatever of benefit could possibly accrue from restrictive navigation laws to Great Britain was especially likely to be manifested.

As the situation of maritime affairs in Great Britain which prompted to the repeal of her navigation laws was not dissimilar to that which now exists in the United States ; and as the arguments offered in the House of Commons and in the English press in opposition to the adoption of a new and liberal commercial policy are so much alike to those now made use of in the United States for the same purpose, that, *mutatis mutandis,* one might almost feel warranted in accusing American speakers and writers of having plagiarized without reserve from their British prototypes of 1849; and as like causes, acting under like conditions, are likely to be followed by the same results in the economic as well as in the physical world,— it will be both profitable and interesting to narrate somewhat in detail, at this point of our discussion, the history and results of British experience.

British Experience of Navigation Laws.

Up to the year 1821, according to a report made to the House of Commons, "no fewer than two thousand laws" had been enacted at different periods for the protection, encouragement, or regulation of British commerce; "every one of which," according to the testimony of McCulloch, which, in turn, was indorsed by Buckle after careful re-investigation, "was an unmitigated evil."

The first British navigation law was passed in 1381, in the fifth year of Richard II., and was substantially what has recently been again commended, in Congress and out, to the American people as a panacea for existing evils; namely, "*that none of the King's liege people should from henceforth ship any merchandise, in going out or coming within the realm of England, but only in ships of the King's liegance,* on penalty of forfeiture of vessel and cargo."

By subsequent enactments, which remained in force until 1849, no foreigner could own, either wholly or in part, a British ship, and the captain and at least three-fourths of the crew of such vessels were compelled to be British subjects. Certain enumerated articles of European produce could only be imported into the United Kingdom, for consumption, in British ships, or in ships of the country of which the goods were the produce. No produce of Asia, Africa, or America could be imported for consumption into the United Kingdom, *from any European port*, in any ships whatever. And such produce could only be imported from any other places in British ships, or in ships of the country of which the goods were the produce. No goods could be carried coastwise from one part of the United Kingdom to another, except in British ships. No goods could be carried from any one British possession in Asia, Africa, or America, to another, in any but British ships. No foreign ships were allowed to trade with any of the British possessions, unless they had been specially authorized to do so by order in council. No goods could be exported from the United Kingdom to any of the British possessions in Asia, Africa, or America (with some exceptions with regard to India), in any but British ships. Again, during the whole of the period of the existence of the British navigation laws, the predominant idea among British statesmen was, that commerce could not take care of itself, that it would decay under the influence of foreign competition, and that legislation — protective and interfering — was the essential thing to make it prosperous. Indeed, it was considered necessary that no Parliament should go out of existence until it had enacted something pertaining to the regulation and encouragement of trade and commerce. "I pray you," said Charles II., in one of his speeches to Parliament, "contrive any good short bills which may improve the industry of the nation ; and so, God bless your councils." Mr. Ricardo, the celebrated economist and author, who wrote before the repeal of the navigation laws, in commenting on this state of things, used the following language, which equally well applies to the existing situation in the United States : "All increase of shipping," he says, "they attributed to acts of Parliament ; none to increase of population and industry and wealth : according to them, all good is the result of restriction and protection, and only evil springs from enterprise and competition. Experience has taught them nothing ; the word 'protection' has so mystified and deluded them that they are martyrs to it, and let it bind them down to inferiority and decay."

"No one," says Mr. W. S. Lindsay, author of a recent work on merchant shipping, "can rise from a study of these laws without a feeling of amazement at the trouble our ancestors gave themselves to 'beggar their neighbors' under the erroneous impression which too long prevailed, that by their ruin our own prosperity would be most effectively achieved. It is therefore not surprising, that, under such legislative measures, maritime commerce

was for centuries slow in growth, and that British merchants and ship-owners frequently suffered quite as much
through the instrumentality of laws meant for their protection as their foreign competitors against whom these
regulations were levelled." [1]

The following details of the experience of British trade
and commerce under these laws will also to some extent
illustrate their absurdity and injurious influence. For
example : —

" An American vessel might carry American cotton to England
direct ; but if such cotton was landed at a Continental port no ship of

---

[1] *Per contra* and as curiously illustrative of how persons discussing public
questions from different standpoints can deduce diametrically opposite conclusions from the same data, attention is asked to the following extract from
a letter written by a leading American statesman, in 1879, to certain merchants of New York City, on the subject of the decay of American commerce,
in which the author specially antagonizes the views of McCulloch, Buckle,
and Lindsay, as above noticed : —

" Let us learn wisdom from our rivals. Not only does England continue
by large pecuniary aids to stimulate the growth of her steam marine, but
from the days of Oliver Cromwell until the reign of Victoria she maintained
the most rigid protection of all her navigation interests. One of our most
intelligent commercial writers and statisticians describes and embodies the
navigation laws of England in words that are always worthy to be quoted : —

"'The laws comprised an ingeniously constructed system in favor of
British seamen, British ship-builders, British ship-owners, and British merchants. The maritime code of Great Britain was proudly entitled by Englishmen "Charta Maritima." No student of history can doubt but that to her
navigation laws England chiefly owes the vast extension of her commerce,
the wonderful development of her national wealth, and that colonial expansion which gave her an empire upon which the sun never sets. Under this
protective policy her power upon the ocean became supreme.' "

any nationality could afterwards land it for consumption in England. The grain of Russia, if once landed in Prussia, or in the ports of any other nation, was absolutely shut out from England, no matter if a deficiency of food in that country was threatening starvation to its people. In 1839 the price of coffee was especially high in the London market. Large quantities of Java and Dutch colonial coffee [1] were in store in Amsterdam, but it could not be brought into England because it had been landed at a Continental port. Under these circumstances it is said that a British ship was chartered, sent to Amsterdam, and despatched to the Cape of Good Hope, where the cargo was landed, actually or constructively, and by some process recognized by the law so became the naturalized produce of that colony. It was then carried to England, and coming direct from a British colony in a British ship was admitted for home consumption. It is said that many thousand tons of merchandise were thus sent cruising half round the globe, involving an enormous waste of capital, in order that the letter of the law might be fulfilled, although its spirit was nullified." — (*Lindsay's History of Merchant Shipping: Hamilton Hill. American Social Science Association, 1878.*)

British legislators, in common with legislators of our own day and nation, were unwilling to learn, except by experience; but, after five centuries of experience in attempting to promote commerce and navigation by law, they began to realize that the general effect of such a

---

[1] In the United States at present (1882) we do not absolutely forbid the importation of Java coffee which has been transported to Amsterdam; but we put a fine of ten per cent of the value of the coffee — i.e., extra duty — if any one undertakes to do such an improper thing, and thus achieve practically the same result as was reached under the more direct and stringent British laws.

policy was injurious and not beneficial. **This** feeling first practically manifested itself in a motion in Parliament, in 1847, by Mr. Ricardo, for the appointment of a committee to inquire into the operation and policy of the navigation laws ; and, although strenuously opposed, the motion was adopted by a vote of 155 to 61. The committee thus created, owing to a termination of the session before they had concluded their labors, never reported ; but the evidence taken by them, and placed on record, abundantly proved that these laws failed to secure superiority either in ships, officers, or crews ; that they failed to secure a supply of seamen for the navy ; that they were prejudicial to both British foreign and colonial trade ; that they caused the enactment by other **countries of similar laws, framed, in** part, for retaliation ; and that they did not secure remunerative profits to the ship-owner. One representative witness, deputed by an association of ship-owners to appear before the committee, expressed the opinion that half the capital embarked in British shipping during the preceding twenty-five years had been entirely lost.

There was, moreover, a **special** stimulus acting on the British mind, at the time **the** reform movement commenced in **1849**, in favor **of a** more liberal maritime policy. Ships **were** then built almost exclusively of wood. The United States could **build** cheaper and better ships than England, **because** the advantage in the material and skill for building was with them. And England, recognizing this fact, felt that **the repeal of** all restrictions in

the way of the purchase by her citizens, of American
ships, was one of the conditions essential to enable them
to meet American competition on the ocean on any thing
like equal terms. (How the United States failed in wisdom
when the conditions were reversed, has already been pointed
out.)   By Act of Parliament, therefore, in 1849, all British
navigation laws of a restrictive character, with the exception of such as pertained to the coasting trade, were repealed ; and, in 1854, the British coasting trade also was
thrown open, without restriction, to the participation of
all nations.   The reason why the British coasting trade
was not also made free in 1849, the same as, and in connection with, British foreign trade, it is now well understood, was because of the unwillingness of the United
States to make any reciprocal maritime concessions.

Although long discussed, and the end, to some extent,
anticipated, this actual abrogation of the British navigation laws finally encountered great opposition throughout
the kingdom ; and predictions were freely indulged in by
such men as Disraeli, Lord Brougham, Lord George
Bentinck, and others, that henceforth "free trade in
shipping would destroy the ship-building trade of Great
Britain, ruin British ship-owners, and drive British sailors
into foreign vessels."   In Liverpool petitions to Parliament against the repeal received 27,000 signatures, while a
counter-petition received only 1,400 signatures.   In London
the petitions against repeal received 23,000 signatures, —
Thomas Baring and other equally influential persons head-

ing the list. **Some leading** British ship-owners, seeing
nothing but ruin before them, sold out their whole tonnage at the best price attainable in a depressed market,
the moment that it became evident to them that all
attempts to further perpetuate the navigation laws would
be useless. In the House of Commons Mr. Disraeli
concluded a long attack upon the first bill repealing the
British navigation laws, in the following words, which
would seem to have served as a model for nearly all
the statesmen of the restrictive school in the United
States from that time onward: "Will you, by the recol-
lections of your past prosperity, by the memory of your
still existing power, for the sake of the most magnificent
colonial empire in the world, now drifting away amid the
breakers, for the sake of the **starving mechanics of Bir-**
mingham and Sheffield, by all the wrongs of a betrayed
agriculture, by all the hopes of Ireland, will you not rather,
by the vote we are now coming to, arrive at a decision
which may to-morrow smooth the careworn countenance
of British toil, give growth and energy to national labor,
and at least afford hope to the tortured industry of a
suffering people?" And he closed by sarcastically ob-
serving that "he would not sing 'Rule Britannia' for fear
of distressing Mr. Cobden, but he did not think the House
would encore 'Yankee Doodle.' He could not share the
responsibility of endangering that empire which extended
beyond the Americas and the farthest Ind, which was
foreshadowed by the genius of Blake and consecrated by
the blood of a Nelson, — the empire of the seas."

Lord Stanley (afterwards Earl Derby), in objecting to the proposal to admit a foreign-built ship to British registry, said, " It was essential to keep up the number and efficiency of our private building-yards, which would speedily decrease in number were such a proposal adopted."

Admiral Martin testified before the select committee of the House of Commons, "that if the abrogation of the navigation laws left the [British] ship-owner at liberty to build his ships in foreign countries, and he availed himself of that license, it would inevitably diminish the shipwright class in this kingdom ; yet on this class the safety of England greatly depended." Mr. Walpole, M.P., said that, "whatever gain might be reaped by individuals, the repeal of the navigation laws would imperil the safety of the country."

Mr. Drummond, M.P., declared "the measure to be the last of a series invented by the Manchester school, the end and intention of which were to discharge all British laborers, and to employ foreign laborers in lieu of them, — foreign sawyers instead of English sawyers, foreign shipwrights instead of English shipwrights, and so on through the whole category of employments." He added "that if there was a satanic school of politics this was certainly it."

The Ship-owners' Society of London, in one of these appeals to Parliament, after expressing the opinion that the maritime greatness of England depended upon the maintenance of the navigation laws, said "that if these laws were abolished 'Rule Britannia' would forever be expunged

from our national songs, the glories of **Duncan and Nelson**
would wither like the aspen-leaf and fade like the Tyrian
dye, and none but Yankees, Swedes, Danes, and **Nor-
wegians** could be found in our ports. Who would there
be to fight our battles, and defend our sea-girt shores?"
Lord Brougham also spoke of the laws that it was proposed to repeal, as having long been considered "not only
as the foundation of our glory and the bulwark of our
strength, but the protection of our very existence as a
nation."

[NOTE. — We fancy some of our readers at this point rubbing their
eyes, and asking themselves if they are not reading from the columns
of some of the leading newspapers of the United States, or from the
speeches of men who have been, or are now, influential in the Federal
Congress.]

But all of these appeals proved powerless to prevent the
progress of reform, and common-sense in the end triumphed by a majority of fifty-six in the Commons and ten
in the House of Lords. Sir Robert Peel, in closing the debate, met the predictions of disaster, so freely indulged in
by the opponents of repeal, by showing that "the same
outcry of ruin to the ship-owner," had always been set up
whenever any measure looking to the unshackling of ocean
trade had previously been proposed ; and adverted in par-
ticular to the circumstance that when in 1782, seventy
years previous, it was proposed to admit Ireland to participation in the colonial trade, the ship-owners of Eng-

land prevented it on the ground that it threatened ruin
to their interests, and that those of Liverpool in a peti-
tion addressed to the House of Commons declared "that,
if any such thing were permitted, Liverpool must be inevitably reduced to its original insignificance."

Experience of British Shipping subsequent to the Repeal of the Navigation Laws.

Let us next inquire as to the results of the experience
of this legislation, and how far the prophecies of doom
indulged in by Disraeli, Brougham, and Drummond were
realized. From 1816 to 1840, the tonnage of the United
Kingdom remained almost stationary, increasing during
the period of twenty-four years to the extent of only 80,-
118 tons. It began, however, to increase immediately
and coincidently with the removal of British protective
duties in 1842, and gained 444,436 tons between 1842 and
1849. After the repeal of the navigation laws it went up
from 3,485,958 in 1849, to 3,662,344 in 1851 ; to 4,284,750
in 1854 ; to 4,806,826 in 1861 ; to 5,694,123 in 1871 ; and
6,574,513 in 1880.[1] But even this statement fails to convey a correct idea of the rapidity of growth which British
commerce has experienced since the shackles for so many
years imposed upon it by the navigation laws were removed ; for, with the introduction of steam as a motive
power for vessels, a very much larger amount of service

---

[1] For the entire empire the aggregate of British tonnage is estimated at a
much higher figure.

is performed with a given amount of tonnage than formerly, thus continually diminishing the necessity for an absolutely large increase of tonnage. For a full understanding, therefore, of what has actually taken place, it is necessary to couple with the statement of the absolute increase of British tonnage a statement of the increase of tonnage entering or clearing the ports of the United Kingdom ; which, comparing 1840 with 1880, has risen from 6,490,485 tons to 41,348,984 tons, — an increase of over 500 per cent.

The statistics of the entries and clearances in the British foreign trade showed an increase in 1860 of 10,000,000 tons over 1850 ; 12,000,000 in 1870 over 1860 ; and 22,-000,000 in 1880 over 1870. British steam-tonnage increased two and a half times during the decade of 1850–60, more than trebled between 1860–70, and increased two and a half times again between 1870-80. " I am not acquainted with any national industry," says Mr. John Glover in a paper on "The Progress of Shipping," read before the Statistical Society of London, February, 1882, "of which such statements could be made on the authority of parliamentary returns." Wooden vessels, according to the same authority, are disappearing from the British register at the rate of about a thousand vessels each year. But, for every ton of effective carrying power thus lost, seven tons through replacement by steamers, it is estimated, are gained. Another curious fact showing the immense economy of steam, brought out by recent investigations, is, that the enormously increased work performed by the British commercial marine in 1880 was performed by fewer hands than were employed in 1870.

The proportion of foreign vessels engaged in the foreign trade of Great Britain in 1850 — the year next after the repeal of the Navigation Laws — was 32.2 per cent; during the next ten years it increased, and was 41.9 per cent in 1860; in 1870 it had decreased to 29.7; and in 1880 it had fallen to 27.8, or 16.2 less than it was in 1850.

As has been already noted, the restrictions on the participation of foreign vessels in the coasting trade of Great Britain were not removed at the time of the repeal of the navigation laws in connection with foreign trade in 1849, but were continued until 1856. Much apprehension was even then felt at the possible effect of the removal of the last British barrier in the way of free ocean commerce; but experience soon showed that freedom was no less beneficial in the smaller sphere of its application than it had proved in the larger. The British coasting trade, as had been the case with the British foreign trade, immediately and largely increased under conditions of freedom; and, while foreign vessels at once and for the first time came in and participated in it, the proportion of the total business transacted by British vessels was greater than ever before, and the superiority once established has never been impaired.

CHAPTER VII.

THE DISCUSSION OF REMEDIES.

HAVING now discussed the inception and primary cause of the decay of American shipping, the nature and influence of our navigation laws, and the experience of other nations — our business competitors — during the period of decay under consideration, the way is now clear for a consideration of the methods and feasibility of bringing back and using ships of the most desirable character as instrumentalities for the profitable employment of the labor and capital of the United States ; and as aids for the accomplishment of what is even yet more important, — namely, the creation or enlargement of markets for the inevitable surplus of the varied products of our industries ; a surplus which threatens at no distant day to be so large, and so undisposable through lack of sufficient foreign markets, as to smother us, as it were, in our own grease.

The First Step in the Way of Recovery.

And first, if the primary cause of the decline of American shipping employed in the ocean carrying trade was due (as beyond all question it was) to the fact that American ships could not do the work which the trade and com-

merce of **the world required to** have done, **as** cheaply, as
expeditiously, and **as** conveniently, as the **ships of** Great
Britain and other **competitive** maritime nations ; **if the
inception of** this decline was coincident with the recogni-
tion **of** this fact by American and foreign merchants ; **and
if the same** causes which in the first instance arrested the
growth and occasioned decay in American ocean tonnage
have ever since continued and are now operative, — then it
needs no argument to prove that the first step to be taken
in the way of recovery, is for the American shipping interest to **put** itself on a par with its foreign competitors,
in respect to the excellence of the tools or instruments —
i. e., the ships and all their appurtenances — which it
needs to employ in the transaction of its business.   Unless this first step can be taken ; unless this primary and
indispensable result can be effected, there is no use of further talking ; and we might as well **fold our** hands, and
complaisantly say, "We do not propose to be a maritime
nation."   People in this age of the world will no more
continue to permanently use poor **or** unnecessarily expensive tools in trade and commerce, than they will in
agriculture and manufactures.   They will either, as the
outcome of intelligence, voluntarily adapt themselves to
the new conditions which may arise, and so prosper ; **or, as**
the outcome of ignorance and obstinacy, adhere to **the old,
and** be crushed and starved out of existence.

The inexpediency **of** denying to citizens **of the** United
States the right to employ such instrumentalities in their

ocean carrying trade as may to them seem best, or essential for withstanding competition, would find an exact illustration, if one of the great trunk lines of railway traversing the United States from the valley of the Mississippi to the seaboard — say, for example, the New York Central — should by reason of statute regulations be constrained to offer inferior accommodations, or establish comparatively higher rates of freights and fares than the Pennsylvania Central. Under such circumstances, it is evident that the former would inevitably lose its business, and decay, and that no legislation or appeal to the State pride of the merchants of New York in favor of their own State road would prevent the decay.

Again, if a man proposing to build a house were told that he must buy his bricks or timber in his own town or State, rather than in some other town or State, and that he would in the long-run suffer no loss by so doing, his answer would probably be, that he individually could judge of that matter better than any one else, and that the only sensible way of deciding the question would be to leave it to him to decide." If at the same time he was asked to contribute to a fund to maintain the business of brick and lumber manufacture in his own town or State, because he desired to use bricks and lumber in the construction of a house, he would soon realize that the whole system of regulating his affairs in accordance with the wishes of the brick and lumber makers was not only an encroachment on his rights, but an almost insuperable

barrier in the way of the development of his business or
interests.   And yet our merchants contentedly listen
with patience, year after year, to statements in respect to
the development of our foreign commerce, by administrators of the government, whose theories and arguments
are inconsistent with the teachings of the most ordinary
and every-day experience.

At this period, furthermore, when the whole tendency
of trade and commerce is to transact business for the minimum of profit on separate transactions, and to aggregate
and increase profits by increasing the number of transactions or the volume of business, it does not require any
large inequality in the way of either profit or loss, as respects different methods, to determine great commercial
results.   Railroad men have found out, for example, that
so small a matter apparently as the civility or neglect of
conductors, or the scarcity or abundance of towels on
sleeping-cars, will sensibly influence the volume of travel ;
and the question as to whether the United States or Great
Britain shall control an export trade of some five thousand millions of yards of cotton cloth, is said by those
who are authority, to turn on a difference in comparative
cost of less than a quarter of a cent a yard.   We start,
therefore, in this discussion of the feasibility of arrest-
ing the decay of American shipping, and promoting its
growth, with the axiom that if the United States proposes to compete for the carrying trade of the ocean, or
expects to carry any considerable proportion even of its

own exports and imports, it must provide itself at the outset with ships in every respect as good and as cheap as
those which its competitors for similar service offer for
employment. The United States at present, it is admitted, has no such vessels; and the question that next presents itself is, How shall they be procured? and the answer is, *Build or buy,* — *one of the two,* — *or go without.*

If we could construct ships in every respect adequate to
meet the requirements of the age, — cost as well as quality
being taken into account, — public sentiment would be
unanimous in favor of doing it in preference to adopting
any other policy. But under existing circumstances we
cannot do it. Certain persons, assuming to speak with
authority, have from time to time, within the last few
years, publicly asserted to the contrary; but the fact that
only *two* iron sailing-vessels have been built in the United
States within the last ten years (1872–82), and these of
only 44 and 36 tons burden respectively, — hardly large
enough for an oyster craft, — and that the trifling amount
of iron steam-tonnage constructed within the same period
has been merely to meet the wants of the coasting trade,
which is forbidden by law to otherwise supply itself, suffi-
ciently prove the falsity of any such averment. What
better testimony under this head, moreover, could be
asked than that furnished by the experience of the line of
transatlantic steamships established some years ago under
the auspices and by the contributions of the Pennsylvania
Central Railroad, to run between Philadelphia and Liver-

pool ; the only transatlantic steamship company which at present (1882) carries the flag of the United States, but which it is now proposed by the subsidizing railroad to discontinue.[1]   At the outset this company proposed to use only steamers of American construction, and did provide itself with four vessels of this character.   But subsequently (1880), finding itself in need of new steamships, it quietly discarded Pennsylvania's pet theories about American industry and employment of home labor, and, being forbidden *to buy* abroad, concluded *to hire* abroad, and so supplied its necessities.

Disuse of Wooden and Sailing Vessels.

Wooden vessels are things of the past, and all the facilities which may be claimed for the United States in respect to the construction of such vessels will therefore count for nothing.   If, in the future revision of our navigation laws in favor of the free purchase and ownership of ships, wooden vessels should be excepted, and, with a view of especially pleasing certain ship-building interests in Maine and other New England States, a provision

---

[1] "The financial results of the American Steamship Company since the commencement of its operations, and the necessity for large outlays for its future maintenance, have caused your Board to doubt the propriety of further diverting your revenues to that purpose ; and to consider the question whether all that could reasonably be asked of your Company on behalf of the commercial interests of this port has not been more than performed, and whether the promotion of steamship lines should not be left to private enterprise." — *Report Penn. Central R. R., March, 1882.*

should be enacted that no citizen of the United States should hereafter purchase or own a wooden vessel of foreign construction, under penalty of death, no American who proposes to use ships as instrumentalities of **commerce** would make the slightest manifestation of protest, except against the combined uselessness and absurdity of the proposition.

It is idle, therefore, to expect relief to our shipping interests by the further fostering of the construction of wooden vessels. About a million and a quarter of American wooden sailing-tonnage is reported as yet engaged in foreign trade , but **it** needs no prophetic gift to foresee that it is doomed **to continuous loss, and destined at no** distant **day to rot at our wharves.** In foreign trade our wooden sailing-vessels have **of late found little opportunity** for employment, except **for the carriage of the mineral oils.** In the coasting business they still maintain a place, principally as carriers of lumber, coal, and other coarse freights ; but even in this field they are every day finding **it more** and more difficult to compete with steam. In the foreign lumber trade of the British Provinces, **steamers** are rapidly supplanting the wooden sailing-vessels ; and no fewer than twenty, some of **them** of nearly 2,000 tons burden, are now engaged in the transportation of lumber from the port of St. John, **N.B.** Again, until within a **few** years past, small wooden sailing-vessels have managed **to** retain a profitable carrying trade between the United States **and the West** Indies and South America. A majority of these vessels were schooners and brigantines of about 120 tons register; some of them expensively fitted up, and designed not only to carry large cargoes, but also passengers. As soon, however, as the swift, cheaply manned, British iron steamer came into this field, the American sailing-vessels began to disappear, as if by magic; and along with the vessels necessarily goes no inconsiderable part of the commerce which they represented. Out of an export and import trade between the United States and Venezuela in 1880, of $8,307,000 valuation, only $3,015,000 was conveyed in American bottoms. The manufacture of wooden vessels in the United States is to-day principally confined to schooners, sloops, yachts, pilot-boats, and other small craft. West of Maine, the building of wooden vessels has practically ceased on our ocean coasts, a circumstance that has to some extent stimulated this business in the above-mentioned State. In the British Provinces a like decadence of wooden sail-tonnage is also noticeable, and the colonial ship-yards are seriously contemplating the abandonment of wood for iron. In Great Britain wood has almost entirely ceased to be a factor in marine construction.

The advantage of iron over wooden sailing vessels is shown by the circumstance, that the former secure a higher classification for a longer term of years, are maintained at less expense, carry more cargo than a wooden ship with an equal displacement up to the construction water-line, obtain higher rates of freights, and even at .

the enhanced rates command the preference of shippers. The main reason of these last advantages is to be found in the difference in the rates of insurance in favor of the iron vessel, and in the less liability of damage to the cargoes by them transported.

Supersedure of Sail by Steam.

But, be the advantage of iron over wooden ships greater or less (and on this point authorities are not fully agreed), it is all but universally conceded, that, except for very long voyages with bulky freights, iron sailing-vessels have also had their day, and will be displaced as rapidly as steamers can be built in substitute. Thus for the year 1880 the building of steamers in Great Britain as compared with sailing-tonnage (mainly iron) was as 6 to 1 ; and, while during the same year the sailing-vessel tonnage of the United Kingdom diminished to the extent of 217,000 tons, the steam-tonnage was increased by 212,000 tons. The loss of sailing-vessel tonnage from the British register during the decade 1870–80 has been estimated at 750,000 tons. It was replaced, however, by an increase of 1,611,-534 steamer tons, with about fivefold increase in carrying capacity.

The following illustration, drawn from the statistics of the carrying trade between the Argentine Republic of South America and Europe, also furnishes a striking illustration of the rapidity with which sail is being supplanted by steam, even in a business in which the carriage one

way is composed almost exclusively of exceedingly bulky
articles as compared with their weight, such as wool, hair,
hides, and sheep-skins. Thus in 1870 this trade was
conducted through the agency of 104 steamers of 144,252
tons, and 1,142 sailing-vessels of 347,304 tons. In 1878
the number of steamers had increased to 244 with 362,542
tonnage, while the number of sailing-vessels had decreased to 547 with only 210,634 tonnage. Again: In
1880, out of the 113,343,000 bushels of grain exported
from New York, 49,966,000 bushels were transported by
1,292 steamers, and 63,376,000 by 1,789 sailing-vessels.
In 1881 the shipments of grain from the same port
were 72,276,000 bushels ; of which 53,265,000 (a gain of
3,289,000) were carried by 1,302 steamers, and only
19,020,000 (a loss of 44,356,000) by 554 sailing-vessels.

But the steamship of ten years ago will not answer the
requirements of the present day. Steamers of recent
construction have been greatly lengthened, increasing
their capacity for freight without proportionally augment-
ing the cost of moving them. The space which the engines and coal take up has been decreased largely, thus
adding to the room for freight. Compound engines with
surface condensers and high measures of expansion are
superseding the engines of former pattern, while the
special feature of British ship-building during the past
two years has been the rapid substitution of steel in the
place of iron for the construction of vessels. If the British anticipations of advantage from the application of

steel should be in even a moderate degree realized, the fact is a matter of no little significance in its bearing on the problem under discussion; for the unquestionably superior facilities which England now enjoys for producing *cheap* steel in large quantities would render competition with her in ship-building in the immediate future far more formidable than it is at present.[1]

Ship-using rather than Ship-construction the Object of Primary Importance to the United States.

In determining under these circumstances what is the best policy for the United States to pursue, it is all-important to endeavor to realize fully at the outset, and keep clearly in view throughout the whole of this discussion, the end and object of primary importance in the way of attainment; and that is, not so much the promotion of

---

[1] A recent English writer, in treating upon the new application of steel to ship-building, illustrates the advantage of this material over iron as follows: Suppose the construction of a transatlantic freight steamer, carrying 3,500 tons (dead weight), is contemplated: "if of iron, the hull will weigh about 2,500 tons, and the entire ship will cost about $350,000; of steel, the hull will weigh 2,000 tons, the total cost being $380,000. Reckoning 6 per cent interest and 6 per cent depreciation, etc., on this $30,000 extra cost, we have $3,600 per annum. As an offset to this the writer estimates as an extra freight on the steel over the iron vessel 500 tons cargo out and 500 tons back. Assuming ten trips per year, this would give 10,000 tons extra freight, which, at $3 average freight per ton, would give $30,000 extra earnings per year. Deducting from this the $3,600, the balance of $26,400 represents the extra net profit per year that would be earned by the steel over the iron steamship, which is equal to $9\frac{1}{2}$ per cent on the entire cost of the vessel."

the business of ship-construction, as that of reclaiming
and repossessing that share in the immense and profitable
business of the ocean transport of freight and passengers
which we formerly possessed, and which as a nation of
the first rank we are entitled to have ; and which, furthermore, we must have if we would enjoy sufficient markets
for the products of our industries, and sufficient opportunity for the profitable employment of our labor.   Hitherto
this distinction has not been appreciated as fully as it
ought to have been ; and mainly for the reason that in-
tentional and persistent efforts have been and are now
constantly being made to befog the whole subject, and
make it appear that the interest of a few persons engaged
in building ships is the first thing to be considered :
while in truth, important and desirable as is the business
of American ship-building, it is most insignificant in comparison with the important results that are certain to
accrue to national wealth from successful ship-owning and
ship-using.

Suppose Congress should be induced to appropriate
$2,000,000 to $3,000,000 to call into existence two or
three lines of steamers to run in competition with non-
subsidized foreign steamers, say between New York and
Liverpool ; their total earnings would not amount to more
than 2½ per cent of the amount which the United States
now annually pays to foreigners for carrying our exports
and imports.   In fact, the clamor which a few individual
owners of ship-yards are making, and the effort that is

being made by others to have it appear that their interest in this matter is paramount, forcibly recalls Patrick Henry's famous old story of John Hook disturbing the American camp with hoarse cries of "Beef! beef!" because it had been found expedient to take two of his steers in order to rescue the Continental soldiers from starvation. There was no doubt that John Hook had lost his steers, and that he ought to have been paid for them ; but this did not prevent the people (according to William Wirt, the biographer of Patrick Henry) from proposing to tar-and-feather him for impudently demanding that his petty claim, rather than the condition of the army, should first receive attention.

The *Policy* of *Common-Sense and of Experience*.

Viewing, then, the case from the standpoint of the relative importance of the several involved interests, and preferring the greater interest to the less, the policy which would seem to be in accordance with all true business principles and also with common-sense, would be for the government to promptly allow every citizen of the United States who desired to purchase and use ships, to freely exercise his own judgment in respect to sources of supply, and not attempt to dictate to him, either directly or indirectly, what kind of ships he shall use, where he shall buy, or how much he shall pay for them. And in recommendation of this policy it should be also borne in mind that the nation is not asked to walk in any new and untried path, but upon a course whose every step is brilliantly illuminated by experience. Thus, for example, it has always been the custom of New-England manufacturers, whose orthodoxy in respect to the protective doctrine has never been questioned, if at any time they hear of a new machine invented or brought into use in Europe, for more effective spinning or weaving, for the carding of wool, or the printing of cloths, or of any new dye, to immediately send and get it ; and keep sending and supplying themselves until American mechanics and chemists, finding a demand existing for the new product, commence to supply it : working tentatively in the first instance, using the foreign article **as a model** or guide, and finally resulting, in most instances, in the production of something better and cheaper than the original. And to such an extent has this policy found favor, **that** Congress in repeated instances has provided that new and improved instrumentalities of production of foreign origin and construction may be imported free of all restriction or duty ; as has been the case with machinery for steam ploughing, for propelling canal-boats, for making beet sugar, **for** the spinning **of** jute, and the like. It **is** obvious that **the** principle conceded in this legislation is identical **with that** involved in the proposed concession of the privilege to freely import ships ; namely, the desire to create or develop a domestic industry through the free importation of **such** instrumentalities **as are necessary for** its successful prosecution, and which instrumentalities at the same time cannot advantageously be obtained in the United States.[1]

Such also was the policy adopted by Great Britain in 1849 (when the United States had demonstrated its superiority in the construction of wooden vessels), by repealing her navigation laws and allowing her merchants and seamen to freely purchase and use the superior American vessels. Such also was the course adopted at a later period by every maritime nation of Europe when English superiority in the construction of iron vessels and steam machinery was demonstrated ; and in no one instance has the result been other than highly advantageous to the purchasing parties and in justification of the liberal policy. The experience of Germany in this connection is exceedingly interesting and instructive. But comparatively few years ago "there was not a machine-shop or a building-yard for iron ships at either of the two great ports of Germany, — Hamburg and Bremen. They possessed a few small ships and barks in the foreign trade, but most of their tonnage consisted of galliots and fishing-smacks which navigated the North Sea ; and it is doubtful if they

---

[1] An attempt has been made to weaken the force of this illustration by asserting that in each instance in which permission for the free importation of machinery has been granted by Congress, it has been difficult or impossible to reproduce it in the United States without a working pattern. The assertion is, however, an absurdity, inasmuch as there is never any difficulty in obtaining models, working-drawings, and specifications of any article offered for sale in a foreign market.

had a dozen captains or officers who were qualified to take command of a steamship. But they had something which we had not, — the liberty to avail themselves as best they could of the new improvements of the age. They were quick to seize upon it. They went to the Clyde, and ordered steamships to be built: they educated their coasting and fishing skippers to the standard required for commanding these, and then took to themselves the whole transatlantic steamship business (i.e., between Germany and the United States), out of which our government defrauded its long-established commercial houses, its educated ship-masters and hardy seamen. The Germans still keep that trade, and each succeeding year increase it, until their flag is known in every considerable seaport on the Western Continent, as well as in the Mediterranean and the isles of the Indian and Pacific Oceans. What an impetus has been given by our supineness to the commercial prosperity of Germany! And have the ship-yards of Bremen and Hamburg suffered any loss thereby? Thousands of people besides the owners and crews of these steamships have been benefited; and to-day there are some of these thousands employed in German ship-yards and machine-shops which would not have had an existence but for the liberal policy of the German government. In these establishments, first made necessary for repairing the fleet purchased for the use of their commerce and employment of their seamen, they have now begun the building of iron steamships (one in 1881 for the Chinese navy); gaining experience by their opportunities for acquiring knowledge in mechanical construction, and thus setting an example from which we might profit." [1]

Again, during the Russian (Crimean) war of 1853–56, the Russian mercantile marine was said to have been entirely destroyed; but during the four years next subsequent to the termination of the war — or between 1856 and 1860 — Russia, with the aid of her former enemy, repaired her losses so rapidly that the amount of her tonnage entering British ports in 1860 was 48 per cent more than in 1850. Had the Russians depended on their own efforts, and through national prejudice refused the co-operation of England, would any such result have been possible? And later, when Louis Napoleon, who as Emperor of the French cannot be charged with any lack of national sentiment, desired to call into existence a Franco-American line of steamships which should cope with the great English lines running to New York, he did not consider that he compromised himself or his people in any way by contracting for the building of the pioneer ships " Ville de Paris " and " Pereire " on the Clyde.

And, finally, we find the Chinese coming late to the appreciation of the desirability of having a commercial marine of the most improved construction, and at the same time recognizing that they had no such vessels, or the means for constructing them. Under such circum-

---

[1] Capt. Codman, *International Review*, February, 1881.

stances, what was the policy of this most sagacious, exclusive, self-reliant people? They interposed no obstacles in the way of the purchase by their merchants of such ships of foreign construction as seemed best suited to their necessities; but at the same time they encouraged and commenced the home construction of vessels of the European type, iron-clads as well as merchant vessels. And under the influence of **this sound** policy, the Chinese commercial and naval fleet has already become one of no small magnitude and importance.

In face, now, of all these lessons of experience, can it be doubted that had Russia, France, Germany, and **China** pursued a policy contrary to what they did adopt, **the** state of their mercantile marine would now be in a condition of depression akin to what exists in the United States, and that the business of the commercial marine of Great Britain would to a corresponding extent have **been** increased? **And could there be any thing** more akin to stark idiocy and insanity than **for a man to** stand up, as did one of the delegates from **New York** City to the Boston Shipping Convention in 1880, and assert "that the entire movement [in the United States] in favor of free ships was in the interest of the British Government, and that the press received pay from the other side of the ocean to advocate this policy in order that all the American ships might be bought out"? [1]

---

[1] Report of Proceedings, Boston Journal.

One further illustration under this **head.** — Would it not be regarded **as** the height of folly for a railway company like the New York Central, for example, with **a press** of profitable business continually offering, **to decline to re- new or** increase its equipment **of** cars **and engines until** the same could be constructed by State artisans and **in State** machine-shops, and for the sole reason that **any** other plan for supplying **the** wants **of trade would** neces- sitate purchases from other artisans and other machine- shops localized in other States, and so be repugnant to State sentiments or traditions? And if some of these other States should happen to be foreign, rather than domestic, would that alone suffice to convert a policy of **confessed** foolishness to one worthy of commendation?

CHAPTER VIII.

Objections to the Repeal of our Navigation Laws stated and considered.

THE objections urged in opposition to the repeal of the navigation laws of the United States, or to the granting of permission to American citizens to purchase and use ships of foreign construction without restriction if they should consider it their interest to do so, may be summarized under the following heads : —

First, That it would fundamentally violate the great doctrine of " Protection," which is at present adopted as the policy of the United States ; and that it would be unjust to withdraw from the domestic ship-building interest that protection against foreign competition which is theoretically extended to every other mechanical industry of the country.

Second, That the end in view, namely, the arrest of the decadence of American shipping, and its restoration to prosperity, can be attained through a system of bounties or subsidies equally well, or better, than by a repeal of the navigation laws.

Third, That a repeal of the navigation laws will not accomplish the desired result.

Repeal of the Navigation Laws a Measure of True Pro-
tection for American Industry.

Under the first head it is to be remarked, that even
accepting to the fullest degree the fundamental principle
of the doctrine of protection to home industry, namely,
that Government should interfere by law to put American
capital and labor as nearly as possible on the same footing as European capital and labor, the proposition to
allow American citizens to purchase ships of foreign construction to be used in the ocean carrying trade ought to
be received with favor. Ships suitable to meet the present requirements of trade and commerce, and constructed
in American ship-yards, cost at present from 30 to 40
per cent more than similar vessels constructed in Great
Britain. It is unnecessary to here inquire as to the
causes of this difference; but only to recognize and accept
the fact, and also that there is no reason to think that
the cause will be speedily removed. To expect that
under such circumstances American ships can compete
with foreign vessels in the same sphere of employment, is
as idle as to expect that a man with his feet in a sack can
compete in a race with one whose limbs are free and un-
shackled. It cannot be done. *The maritime countries of*
the world which will do the business which the world
requires to be done upon the ocean cheapest will get and
keep the business; and if we would now retrace our steps,
and get back what we have commercially lost, or rather

have thrown away by **our** amazing folly and short-sighted-
ness, **we** have got to keep this one point primarily and
steadily in view, and make it the basis of our future
policy.[1]

To repeal the prohibition against the purchase of foreign ships is not therefore a free-trade measure, in the
sense in which that term is generally used, but a measure
in the largest interest of protection. **It is** a measure, not
so much with a view of setting our commerce up, as for
removing an obstacle to its setting itself **up.** It is a genuine American policy according to the doctrine **of** protection, inasmuch as it will tend to promote and develop a

---

[1] The American consul at Naples, in a recent report to the State Department, furnishes the following practical illustration of the truth of this proposition. Alluding to the recent notable increase of foreign vessels engaged
in the trade between American and Mediterranean ports, he says, " All these
foreign vessels engaged in the carrying trade between the Mediterranean and
the United States show that there is no want of business. But the trouble is,
our vessels are not able to compete with them for it, for the very simple
reason that it costs an American ship-owner more to build or buy and run a
vessel than it does a foreigner. For this reason it was that Mr. —— of New
York had to run his fruit-steamers last year under the English flag instead of
under the American. The effort to protect our few ship-builders by not permitting our merchants to buy ships abroad has simply had the effect of preventing a return of our commercial prosperity without benefiting our ship-builders;
for our few vessels, built by them at a greater cost, cannot compete in the
carrying trade with vessels that cost less. While foreign steamers and sailing-vessels are continually finding cargoes in Naples and other Italian ports
for New York, our vessels are very frequently returning in ballast, after dis-
charging their cargoes of petroleum or tobacco, because they cannot afford to
accept the rates offered for carrying fruits, marble, sulphur, rags, etc."

great branch of domestic industry, while the **present**
policy, which pretends to be genuine, is really **promotive**
of European interests; and finally, but not least, it is a
protection that is to accrue by the taking-off, and not by
the imposing, of restrictions and **taxes.**

But some may ask, Is there not an enormous injustice
involved in subjecting to a high rate of duty every thing
imported that enters into the composition of steamers
and ships, — such as iron, brass, boiler-plates, rivets, copper, crockery, bedding, wire, cordage, anchors, etc., — and
then allowing the vessels themselves, all equipped and
composed of these same articles, to be imported free of all
duty? The answer to this is to be found in the circumstance that the commodities **above specified, when im-**
ported separately, are for use in a protected market, while
the ship as a whole is **to be used in an** open and unpro-
tected market in competition **with** ships that are not burdened with taxes on their constituent materials. In the
home and protected market, if the manufacturer of cloth
or of hardware is obliged, for the sake of protecting or
favoring the domestic iron and steel industries, to pay more
for **his metals or his** machinery, **he can** recoup himself
by adding the **tax** or advance to the prices of his finished
product, when **the** burden is transferred to the domestic
consumers, **who, as they cannot** avail themselves of any
other market or more favorable conditions, have to bear it.
But **when** an American citizen, employing vessels burdened with an undue **cost,** undertakes to compete on the

open ocean with foreign vessels constructed at some 30 to 40 per cent less cost, he cannot in any way recoup himself on his customers for his disadvantage, for the rate at which the cheaper class of vessels can afford to perform the service required will determine the rate for all. "The vessel launched upon the Delaware and the vessel launched upon the Clyde compete upon precisely the same conditions upon the broad arena of international commerce." In short, the American sailor and ship-owner engaged in foreign trade are so situated that they experience all the burdens of the tariff and nothing of its protection. There is protection for an infinitude of other manufacturing and business interests of much less importance to the country, ranging all the way from 10 to 150 per cent; but for the manufacture of ships, and particularly steamships, to be employed in the foreign carrying trade, there is not only no protection, but a heavy and discriminating imposition of burdens. How heavily the existing tariff (1882) lays its hand upon the American ship-building and ship-using interest at every point, is clearly shown by the following table : —

TAXES ON SOME OF THE PRINCIPAL MATERIALS USED IN STEAMSHIP MANUFACTURE UNDER THE EXISTING TARIFF.

Wrought iron for ships and steam-engines, 2
  cents per pound   .   .   .   .   .   . 18 p. ct. *ad valorem.*
Cables and cable chains, $2\frac{1}{2}$ cents per pound   . 56 "   "
Anchors and parts of anchors, $2\frac{1}{4}$ cents per
  pound   .   .   .   .   56 "   "

Boiler and other plate iron, 25 dollars per ton . 69 p. ct. *ad valorem.*
Nails and spikes, 1½ cents per pound .   . 37 " 　"
Cast-iron steam-pipes, 1½ cents per pound . 47 " 　"
Rolled or hammered iron, 1¼ cents per pound . 54 " 　"
Screws, for wood, 8 to 11 cents per pound . . 50 " 　"
Sheet-iron, 1¼ to 3 cents per pound   .   . . 51 " 　"
Copper sheathing, 3 cents per pound .   . . 26 " 　"
Wire rope, strand, or chain, 2 cents per pound
　and 15 per cent   .   .   .   .   .   . 57 " 　"
Wrought rivets and bolts, 2½ cents per pound . 44 " 　"
Wrought steam and water tubes, 3½ cents per
　pound   .   .   .   . 67 " 　"
Steel in forms not otherwise specified .   . . 30 " 　"
Tarred cable and cordage, 3 cents per pound . 26 " 　"
Manilla (untarred) cable, 2½ cents per pound . 26 " 　"
Other descriptions, untarred, 3½ cents per pound . 24 " 　"
Sail duck, or canvas for sails   .   .   . . 30 " 　"
Tar and pitch   .   .   .   . 20 " 　"
Plank, deals, and other sawed lumber of hemlock,
　1 dollar per 1,000 feet.
Timber for spars .   .   .   . 20 " 　"

And, as typical of this whole system, it may be further noted, that the American flag, — which symbolizes our sovereignty and our commerce, — through the taxes imposed on the bunting of which it is composed, is comparatively one of the most costly luxuries that a citizen of the United States can indulge in ; the tariff on the importation of bunting, levied for the benefit of mainly one corporation in New England, ranging from 77 to 132 per cent *ad valorem.*

And if to these and other taxes are taken into account the State and municipal taxes on the finished ships and their constituents, our excessive tonnage, clearance and harbor dues, compulsory pilotage, and the like, one soon ceases to wonder why American shipping — apart from the coasting trade — is practically a thing of the past, and why even the coasting trade, protected as it is from all foreign competition, does not flourish and hold its own.

But, interesting as this discussion may be from a theoretical point of view, it is at present of little practical importance; for as the United States are building no ships for employment in foreign trade, never have built any in recent years except as experiments, and are never likely to under existing laws which offer a premium " not to do it," there is no substantial existing ship-building interest to protect. What is called the great American industry of ship-building is at present but the interest of a very few individuals, — mainly iron-ship builders, — whose solicitude about the condition of our commercial marine does not extend beyond the limits of their own ship-yards, and whose impudence and persistency in demanding that they shall have employment, though our ocean tonnage in the mean time becomes extinct, borders closely on the sublime.

No Rational Defence of our Navigation Laws possible.

. Finally, those who oppose the repeal of the present navigation laws on the ground that it is necessary to

maintain them in order to protect American ship-building, encourage commerce, promote national independence,
and educate a large body of skilful seamen ready for any
emergency, find themselves confronted with the disagreeable and undisputed facts, that, under the influence of
these very laws, our ship-yards have become deserted, our
ocean carrying trade has dwindled to insignificance, while
an American sailor has come to be regarded almost in the
light of a curiosity. In short, every end for which the
navigation laws were originally instituted has been frus-
trated ; and no result following their repeal could be any
worse than what exists, or is certain to follow their continuance.

Another result of the present state of things, which, if
it has not already happened in a degree, is certainly to be
apprehended in the future, is the destruction, through the
shutting-out of free competition with foreign ship-builders,
of the inventive faculty of our nautical engineers and mechanics. American genius in days past has led the way
in many great improvements in marine architecture ; but
with the decline of our ocean marine, the shutting-up of
our yards, and the continuance of antiquated, obstructive
laws, we seem to offer no longer any incentive to either
genius or enterprise in this direction. Bring back the
ships, even by buying them abroad, and the repairs of a
large merchant marine on this side of the Atlantic, which
cannot be avoided, will afford more employment to labor,
and require the use of more capital, than ship-building in

the United States now does or ever can under the existing system. We must be a large ship-using, before we
can be a large ship-building, nation. And, in respect to
the plea so frequently urged about the claims of home
labor in ship-building, it should be remembered that more
wages are probably disbursed to sailors in a single week
in the little of the ocean marine that is still left to us than
all the ship-builders in the country — iron and wood —
now pay their operatives in an entire year.

Proposed Revival of American Shipping by means of Subsidies.

Second, But it is claimed that the decadence of American shipping can be arrested, and an era of maritime prosperity inaugurated, in some other and better manner than
by the repeal of the navigation laws ; that is, by the payment of bounties or subsidies. Or in other words, having
almost completely destroyed a great branch of domestic
industry by compelling it to submit to the unnatural
restraints of an artificial system, it is now proposed to
repair the damage, not by removing the cause, but by
resorting to another artificial expedient, namely, the
hiring of men to do what the first artificial system (which
it is proposed to continue) makes it for their interest not
to do. On its very face, could any proposition be more
economically monstrous and unpractical ? But, discarding
all matters of sentiment, let us examine the proposition in
question from a purely practical point of view.

The first objection to this scheme is, that it is a mere palliative, and even if remedial in part, and unobjectionable as a matter of public policy, bears no proportion to the magnitude of the trouble to be dealt with. It is a **good** deal like the old method of using perfumes to cover up the results of organic nastiness, or of bathing a swollen limb with liniment when it is a fractured bone that needs setting. Suppose the government should appropriate several millions of dollars to compensate several American-built lines of steamers for running at a loss in competition with steamers of foreign construction. Undoubtedly this policy would benefit the lines so subsidized. Capitalists can unquestionably be bribed to float the American flag to a certain extent. But how about all the rest of our commercial marine that is threatened with annihilation? Does anybody suppose, with the present temper of a large proportion of the American people in respect to subsidies, protection, and the expenditure of public moneys raised by taxation, that the policy of paying bounties can be continued indefinitely as to both time and amount? But they must be so continued **on** the bounty theory, unless the causes which will not allow citizens of the United States to build and use ships as cheaply as foreigners, are removed; and if they are removed their bounties will no longer be necessary, for ships then will be procured without bounties. The application of bounties is therefore a mere temporizing policy, and does not meet the broad problem, how to prevent the transfer of

our whole ocean service to foreigners. What the country
needs is a system that will enable it to run steamships
everywhere on the ocean, in successful competition with
those of other countries.   It wants such a system at once,
before the existing ruts of commerce which now turn
away from the United States have become any further
deepened, and mercantile habits and alliances adverse to
our interests, which have all the force of the law, are
further established.   In these days, when space and time
are no obstacles to the intercourse of nations, when international barriers, formerly so obstructive to trade, are
being rapidly removed, days and weeks count as much in
the world's business as months and years once did ; and
the United States cannot afford to wait for the slow construction of the few ocean lines of steamers that it is
proposed to put in operation under the subsidy system.
" Why don't you file a crowbar down to a needle?" asked
a Chinese woman of a New-England missionary.   " Because it takes too long, and is not the fashion in this age
of steam," was the reply.

Again : our whole experience in respect to the payment of bounties or subsidies as a method of encouraging
ocean navigation has been unfavorable.   The Federal exchequer for years was opened in order that that mode of
developing our steam-marine might have a fair trial ; and
to-day what do we see?   Hardly a solitary United-States
steamship in the transatlantic carrying trade ; and New
York, Boston, Philadelphia, Baltimore, and New Orleans,

to all intents and purposes, not American, but British, German, French, Italian, and Scandinavian ports.

Before the war, the government contributed largely in way of subsidies to the Collins, Havre, Bremen, Pacific, and other lines, but these contributions had no effect in preventing the continued decay of our commercial marine; and in 1860–61 there were no ocean mail-steamers, away from our coasts, under the American flag, with the single possible exception of a line of two vessels between New York and Havre.

From 1867 to 1877, when there was no war or Confederate cruisers to interfere with the development of our commerce and the use of American ships, the United States paid still larger sums in the way of subsidies; in the aggregate, $4,750,000 to the Pacific Mail Steamship Company, and $1,812,000 to the line between the United States and Brazil. The system as an agency for restoring our commercial marine had, therefore, during this period of eleven years, as fair a trial as possible; and the results it worked out so far failed to accomplish what its advocates had in view, and were connected with such a disgraceful chapter of Federal legislation, that from that day to this, Congress and the country, as if disgusted with the record, have indignantly set their faces against the whole system, and few, save those who have had special interests to promote, have come forward to urge its revival.

Doubtless the payment of bounties to American ship-

ping would be productive of one desirable result, besides
benefiting the owners of the vessels who are to be the
recipients; namely, it would prevent our flag from being
absolutely driven from the ocean. But how much will
the country be likely to be called upon to pay for such a
result? "The New-York Commercial Bulletin" has recently made an approximative estimate. Judging from
the provision, in the subsidy bills recently presented to
Congress, about $35 per ton will ordinarily be required to
enable the American-built steamer to compete with the
foreign. "At this rate," says "The Bulletin," "each
vessel of 3,000 tons would require a subsidy income of
about $105,000 a year; ten such vessels would need
$1,050,000; and an addition of 100,000 tons to our ocean
tonnage would call for a subsidy of $3,500,000. Now, as-
suming the people to be willing to absolutely throw away
$3,500,000 for the mere glory of the thing, how much
glory would they get for that expenditure? Our 100,000
tons would be equal to less than 4 per cent of the present ocean steam-tonnage of Great Britain, our great competitor!"

Let us consider, furthermore, from a business and not a
sentimental standpoint, what is to be gained by subsidies
to shipping? It will not be contended that ocean freights
are in consequence to be made cheaper. That is not the
point; but it is claimed that Americans will thereby be
able to participate to a greater extent than they now do in
the business of ocean transportation. They cannot now do

so at a profit with the expensive ships that **they** must use,
or go without : consequently, any profit they are to make
under **the subsidized system must** be derived **from the**
subsidies, or, what is the same thing, taxes, for subsidies
mean increased taxes. The subsidy scheme really comes
down, then, to a proposition that the people of the country
should be further taxed, without the prospect of any corresponding benefit. What answer is the agricultural portion of our people, who furnish more than eight-tenths of
all the exports of the country, likely to return to such a
proposition ? Is it at all probable that they will consent
to be taxed in order to have their cotton, provisions, and
cereals **carried** at one and the same rate in a home-built
vessel in preference to a foreign one ? If the policy of
granting subsidies would lead to the establishment of lines
to parts of the world with which the United States has
now no regular and direct communication, something
might be said in its favor. But such routes are the very
last which the subsidized vessels will select; for the
commercial policy of the United States, other than that involved in the navigation laws, stands in **the way of** American vessels obtaining freights upon many desirable ocean
routes, both in **going** and returning, and under such **cir-**
cumstances lines subsidized at the rate **of even** $35 per
ton could not long maintain themselves. It seems clear,
therefore, that subsidies as **a means** of restoring Ameri-
can shipping cannot **be made the** policy of the United
States, and that, as it is idle **to look for** remedies in this

direction, valuable time and great opportunities should be no longer wasted in discussing it.

Has the Commercial Marine of Great Britain and other Maritime Countries been built up and sustained by the Agency of Subsidies, or Extraordinary Payments of Money on the Part of the State?

Prominent among the arguments brought forward in support of the proposition to attempt to arrest the decay and restore the prosperity of our commercial marine by means of subsidies, or extraordinary payment on the part of the Government, is the assertion, *that the systematic appropriation of large sums for the special object of encouraging ship-using and ship-building* has always been the practice and **policy** of Great Britain; and, further, that through the continuance and present maintenance of such a system is to be **attributed** in great **part the** continued advance and present **great** development **of the** British **shipping** interest. So frequently and so unqualifiedly, moreover, have these assertions been made during recent years **on** the floor of Congress, by public officials, by Chambers of Commerce, and by leading journals,[1] and

[1] "England, **feeling** her advantage and eager to push it, did not leave her commerce to its **own** development, even **with** all the elements in her favor; but she stimulated **its** growth by enormous bounties paid to those who would **build** and sail steamships." "**A** current misrepresentation is to the effect **that** European countries, having **realized the** impolicy of **aiding** steamship lines **of** money subsidies, have **abandoned** it. Just the reverse is the truth." — *Letter of Hon. James G. Blaine to the Merchants of New York, June,* 1879.

so seldom have they been questioned, that the people
of the United States have very generally come to regard
them as matters of history and of record, which could not
be doubted; and, the premises being once accepted, the
conclusion was legitimate, that for the Federal Government to adopt the subsidy system was but to follow a
policy which the long experience of the greatest maritime
nation of the world had taken out of the domain of theory,
and proved to be eminently wise, practicable, and successful. All these assertions, however, will be found on
examination to rest upon no truthful or substantial basis;
and are what may be properly designated as "historic
lies," originating mainly, in the first instance, without
intent to deceive, through an imperfect understanding of
the subject, and subsequently repeated and given credence
on the basis of some personal and supposed trustworthy
authority, without any attempt to inquire further as to
their accuracy.

In support of this averment, attention is asked to the
following statement of facts:—

In the annually published fiscal exhibit of the British
Government, an item of expenditure always appears in

"In addition, it is found that Great Britain, with a keen perception of the
incalculable advantage and benefit it is to her people to attain the supremacy
of the ocean, has led up to it by a system of subsidies; and it is well known
and authenticated that for many years that country has not only aided in its
development, but maintained the existence of its commercial lines by a
system of subsidies."— *Report Special Committee New-York Chamber of
Commerce,* "*On American Shipping,*" *January,* 1882.

the accounts of the Post-Office Department, under the head of "*Packet Service;*" and which, in the absence of any similar expenditure on the part of the Federal Government, seems large to a citizen of the United States; the gross aggregate ranging from £1,138,700 ($5,693,500) in 1872, to £884,054 ($4,420,270) in 1876, and £710,514 ($3,552,570) in 1882.

In the recent discussions which have taken place on this subject in the United States, the inference and assertion are both often made, that this item of expenditure represents the amount of subsidy or bounty which Great Britain annually pays to her steamship lines for their support or encouragement, irrespective of the cost of her postal service.[1] Such, however, is not the case. Great Britain does not subsidize[2] (using the term in the sense of bounties or premiums) any of her steamship lines.

---

[1] "This very year, besides a liberal allowance for sea-postages, Great Britain is paying her various steamship lines a subsidy exceeding $3,700,000, or, to *quote* accurately from the appropriation of Parliament, £767,877." — *Letter by Hon. James G. Blaine to the Merchants of New York, June* 17, 1879.

[2] To one who proposes to investigate this subject himself, some confusion may result from the different sense in which the term "*subsidy*" is used in the United States and England. In the former, the term is generally regarded as equivalent to a "bounty," or "premium," to encourage, or as compensation disproportionate to the ordinary commercial value of the service rendered. In England, on the contrary, as in Lindsay's "Merchant Shipping," the term is not exclusively used in the sense of a bounty, but is applied indifferently to any payment by the government for its ocean mail-service.

The amount charged under the head of "packet service," in her fiscal exhibits, simply represents compensation for carriage of ocean mails for the United Kingdom, the colonies, and foreign governments, and is not additional to such payments ; and any inference that such expenditures partake in any degree of the nature of bounties is as unwarranted as would be the supposition that the amounts likewise annually expended by Great Britain for ordnance, armor-plates, or cavalry-horses, are, in all or part, for the purpose of encouraging her miners, iron-workers, or stockraisers. Furthermore, the expenditures annually charged to the account of packet service, in the returns of the British Post-Office Department, represent only the gross amounts paid, without regard to certain repayments received from the colonial governments, and from other countries where letters are in part carried by the English mails. These repayments usually amount to about two-thirds of the gross sum charged under the head of British Postal Expenditures, and are credited under the head of Post-Office and Miscellaneous Receipts. Thus, for example, in 1872 Great Britain paid in gross £984,625 to various steamship companies for her whole foreign mail, or "packet" service; but of this sum £210,839 was reimbursed by the colonies, and £442,095 by other countries; leaving £332,700 as the net payment by the government for that year on account of purely British postage. And in later years the amount of this item has been very considerably reduced. It will thus appear, that, instead of Great Britain having paid nearly $5,000,000 in 1872 as subsidies to her ocean steamship lines, her net expenditures were only about one-third that amount ; and that was not in any sense as subsidy, but under contracts made by the Post-Office Department, solely upon considerations affecting the efficiency and economy of the mail-service. The fact, also, that all such contracts are always made after public advertisement and public competitive tenders on the part of all who may desire to participate in the service, excludes the possibility of there being any thing in them in the nature of a benefaction or bounty, which could alone be authorized by a direct and specific enactment by Parliament.

A word next in explanation of this so-called " packet service " of Great Britain, which finds no exact counterpart in the administrative machinery of the Federal Government. For two hundred years, and more, Great Britain has maintained a system of colonies, and military ports, all over the surface of the globe; and it has been both a political and military necessity to that government, that communication between her vast foreign dependencies (now embracing some 200,000,000 of population) and the mother-country, by means of ocean ship-service, should be constantly and efficiently kept up. The expense of such a policy has obviously at all times been very considerable ; and as some of the British colonies and military stations are without the direct lines of the world's commerce, it has been found necessary in some special cases to pay comparatively large sums for the sake of securing regular communication with them. But no one ever thought of regarding such payments in the days of sailing-vessels as in the nature of subsidies for the encouragement of commerce and ship-building.

At the outset this entire service was necessarily performed by sailing-vessels, partially under government and partially under private ownership; and as political considerations at that time entered into this matter of ocean mail transportation, the supervision of the whole business was intrusted to the Admiralty, while the expenditures incurred were aggregated and voted by Parliament under the general head of " Naval Estimates." In 1821 the British Government undertook to do this work mainly with its own vessels, and accordingly established regular lines under the title of the " British (Ocean) Packet Service;" but the experiment proved so costly, that after twelve years' experience, or in 1833, it was abandoned, and the system of private contract was mainly substituted. When ocean steam-navigation became a possibility, the same policy was continued.

It is not to be denied that at the outset Great Britain paid much more for her ocean steamship service that she has in later years, and for the same reason that she would have had to pay $140 per ton for Bessemer steel in 1867, which she can now buy for $30; namely, it cost more. Up to about 1851–52 the problem whether any ocean steamship could be navigated with profit was a doubtful

one; and it may be admitted, that, foreseeing how the
union of all the parts of her widely extended empire
would be enormously strengthened by its successful solu-
tion, Great Britain for a term of years paid more than
the actual mail-service rendered her by the steamers was
worth, in order to promote it. But, if such were her
motives, the result sattained were not exclusive, but were
open to all the world to profit by; and the Americans,
coming in later into the business, did so far profit by
them, that in 1851 the foreign steamship tonnage of Great
Britain and the United States was almost equal, that of
the former being 65,900 tons, and that of the latter
62,300.

In 1851, the problem of the success of ocean steamship
navigation having been favorably decided, Mr. John Inman,
possessing no more information or facilities than were
available to other competitors, started his line of transatlantic screw steamers, which were to carry general
cargo and emigrant passengers, and to be independent in
all respects of either the British Admiralty or the Post
Office; and from that time to this there has been a
constant succession of other lines put in operation which
have been pre-eminently successful, and which have never
received government aid of any kind, not even compensation for ocean postal service. And these facts, which cannot be questioned or denied, conclusively demonstrate the
unsoundness of the assertion, on the one hand, that the
present great development and supremacy of British ocean

steam-navigation is due to the continued payment of bounties by the government; and, on the other, **that** government aid in the way of subsidies (bounties) is and has been necessary for the resuscitation of the American commercial marine, unless it is at the same time assumed **that** the Americans are an inferior race, and are unable to do under equal circumstances what the Englishman has found no difficulty in accomplishing. And, if circumstances have not been equal, it is because our navigation laws and fiscal policy would not permit it, and for no other reasons. But let us now go back, and follow up more particularly the policy of the British Government in respect to her ocean mail and transport service from the year 1833, when the exclusive government packet service was abandoned, and the system of private contracts adopted. The business, as before stated, was continued under the charge of the Admiralty, and was neither wisely nor economically conducted. The contracts, it was alleged, were not awarded impartially; and the cost of the service was greatly in excess of the postages received. **The** extent of the expenditures, from the fact that they were included under the **head of naval appropriations**, did not for a long time attract public attention; **but in** 1859–60 Parliament took up the matter, and commenced an investigation. An attempt was made to exculpate the Admiralty on the grounds that its large outlays had been **the** indirect means of encouraging commerce **and** creating **a steam-marine available** in **case of war.** But the plea

was not satisfactory to Parliament; and in 1860 it rebuked
the management of the Admiralty by transferring the
whole ocean mail-service to the Post Office, abolishing the
system of private contracts, and throwing the whole business open to public competition. And such, from that
day to this, has been the British system. Under it no
more is paid than a fair commercial price for the service
rendered to the government; and the fact of public tender
for the service, as before stated, necessarily excludes the
idea of any gratuity.[1] The British Government also
never hesitates to employ foreign lines of steamers when
equal service or cheaper terms can be obtained from
them, as has been the case with the American Pacific
Mail line. Furthermore, the value of the payments
which the British Government does make to ocean
steamship lines for its mail-service are much diminished by the strict requirements which it makes in
respect to construction, equipment, and general management of the vessels employed. To most, if not all, of its
contracts, heavy penalties are attached for the non-per-

---

[1] "There is no evidence before us, that, during recent years at least, Great
Britain has sought to promote ship-building by the direct payment of bounties or subsidies. She has removed all duties upon articles entering into
the construction of ships or necessary for their outfit, or to be used and
consumed by them at sea. She has also repealed all restrictions upon the
purchase of vessels abroad; and thus, by the application of the healthful
stimulus of foreign competition, she has quickened the energies and capabili-
ties of her ship-builders to the very utmost." — *Report National Board of
Trade* (*United States*), 1880.

formance of stipulations; and these penalties are understood to be rigidly exacted. Thus the Peninsular and
Oriental Company is subjected to a penalty of $500 for
every twelve hours in excess of the contract time between
Brindisi and Bombay on outward voyages, and $1,000 for
every twelve in such excess on the homeward voyage.
On the Cape of Good Hope Line, when the voyages exceed the contract time by three days, heavy penalties are
incurred for one or more of these days; and for every complete hour in addition, £6. 5s. is exacted. In the service
between Dover and Calais, a deduction of £5. is made if
a steamer is fifteen minutes late; and for the service
between Holyhead and Kingstown, which includes the ex-
pedition of the mails to and from the United States, there
is a penalty of £1. 14s. a minute if the trips between
London and Kingstown, Ireland, exceed the stipulated
limit.

But perhaps nothing better in the way of helping to an
understanding of this subject can be offered, than to ask
the attention of the reader to a record of practical experience under the British system, — a record extending over
the whole period of years covered by this controversy, and
so full and capable of verification as to leave no opportunity for doubt or disputation. One of the greatest and
most important of the British steamship lines is that
known as the "Peninsular and Oriental Company," which
carries the mails, government despatches, and messengers
weekly between England, Gibraltar, Malta, and Alexan-

dria, with a special line from Brindisi in Italy to Suez
and back, in connection with a rapid overland mail
through France and Italy. From Suez, lines of steamers
run to Bombay, Galle, Ceylon, from whence other lines
diverge to Madras and Calcutta, to the various ports of
Australia, to Singapore, China, and Japan ; a most varied
service, most important to the government in view of its
political and trade relations with India and China, and
involving great expenditure. If there ever was an instance, therefore, in which it would seem that the British
Government would and ought to have supported a line
by subsidies, — using the term in the sense of payments
disproportionate to the commercial value of the service
. rendered, — we would expect to here find it.

But what are the facts ? The line had its inception
about the year 1825, in a small shipping venture started
by two young men, — Messrs. Wilcox and Anderson, — with
a few sailing-vessels and with but little capital or influence. By plodding and intelligent industry they gradually earned success ; and when the ocean steamship was
introduced they established, in 1834, a line of steamers
between London and Spain. Previous to 1837 the government mails between London, Cadiz, and Gibralter were
conveyed by government sailing-vessels and a steam-
packet. The steamers of Messrs. Wilcox and Anderson
being more efficient, the proprietors offered their services
to the government for the transportation of letters ; but
so far from the government exhibiting any interest in the

new enterprise, their proposals were for a considerable time coldly and almost contemptuously disregarded; and it was not until 1837, and after loud complaints on the part of the public at the inefficiency of the official service, that government thought it expedient to inquire of the managers of the Peninsular steamers if they had plans or proposals to submit. They did submit proposals, and they were favorably considered; but here comes in a bit of history which throws a flood of light on the past policy of the British Government, which is held up as an example for the United States to follow.

Thus the proposals of the Peninsular Company were, as before stated, received with favor by the government; but at the same time the company was informed that no private contracts would be made, but that the service must be put up to public competition. And an advertisement was accordingly issued, **inviting tenders** from all owners of steam-vessels for the conveyance of the mails between England and Cadiz, in conformity with the plans submitted by the Peninsular Company; so that the managers of this "struggling undertaking," says Mr. Lindsay,[1] "had to compete against others for the performance of this service, though on plans drawn up by themselves at the request of the government."

Another company submitted bids more favorable than the Peninsular and Oriental, and for a time had prefer-

[1] Lindsay (W. H.), " History of Merchant Shipping," London, 1876.

ence ; but, failing to comply with the stipulations, the contract was again advertised, and again thrown open to the
public, when the Peninsular and Oriental Company took
it, but only on condition of reducing their original bid, on
demand of the government, from £29,600 to £20,500.
And this was in 1837, when ocean steam navigation was
a doubtful experiment, and when, according to the advocates of the adoption of the bounty system by the Federal
Government, Great Britain was assiduously building up
her commercial steam-marine by the generous appropriation of enormous subsidies.   So far, furthermore, was this
from being the case, that in the early days of steam navigation the British Government rarely, and perhaps never,
took the initiative in respect to new projects for ocean
transport, or did any thing whatever for their encouragement, until absolutely driven to it by the force of dissatis-
fied public opinion.[1]

---

[1] The case of the Cunard Company is frequently adduced as an example
to the contrary.   The facts are, however, as follows : The idea of this line
originated with Mr. Samuel Cunard, a citizen of Halifax, N.S.   It received
its first government business, as the most favorable bidder, under public
advertisement, by the Admiralty in 1838, for proposals for the conveyance of
the North American mails by steamers.   The original contract was for the
performance of two voyages a month, and three steamers, for £55,000 per
annum.   Subsequently the Admiralty required four vessels, and the payment
was increased to £81,000 per annum.   The government required the vessels
to be built after their own specifications and under their inspection ; and it
was also provided that the vessels might be used by the Admiralty in time of
war, and that they should carry officers of the British navy.   Subsequently,
when the Cunard Line had been established, and made a success, great com-

Such, then, was the origin of the great Peninsular and Oriental line of steamers. The proprietors gradually extended their business, and finally stretched out to India, and superseded the old lines of sailing-vessels and steam-packets maintained by the Government and the East India Company for mail and other government service. But it was hard work all the time for the company to obtain extended opportunities for service from the government. Thus, in 1839, the India mails, between England and Alexandria, were transported in the main by government packets, and required from three weeks to a month for the performance of the single trip. And, "imperfect as was this mode of transportation, it would probably have continued many years, had not circumstances occurred rendering an alteration imperative;" which were the entering into a convention by the British Government with France in 1839 for the sending of letters to and from India through

---

plaints were made, that the public was taxed for a service from which one company alone profited; that the service could be performed at far less expense than was incurred; and that a monopoly had been created by the Government to the great injury of other steamship-lines engaged in the same trade, or who were desirous of entering it; and under such circumstances Parliament ordered an official investigation. A committee of the House of Commons accordingly investigated, and in 1846 reported that the terms of the contract with the Cunard Company were more advantageous than any others that could then be made by the Government, and that the service had been most efficiently performed. And here ended in Great Britain all further talk about government monopolies and disproportionate payments in respect to this line.

France, by way of Marseilles, and from thence to Malta
and Alexandria by admiralty packets. The plan worked
badly; and this fact, together with the circumstance "that
the British despatches ran some risk of loss in their
transit through France," compelled the government to
seek some quicker and different means of conveyance of
the mails. The managers of the Peninsular and Oriental
Company again came forward, and submitted proposals for
the establishment of a line of superior steamers between
England and Alexandria, at a cost not exceeding what was
required for the maintenance of the small and inefficient
admiralty packets. The tender was, however, received
with reluctance. Many people of influence, says Mr.
Lindsay, threw their influence against it, and almost con-
vinced the government of the desirability of again transporting all the mails by the old way of the Cape of Good
Hope; and it was only after the Peninsular and Oriental
Company had bid lower for the service than all others,
and had proposed in addition to convey all officers travel-
ling on public service at reduced rates, and admiralty
packages gratuitously, that their offer was accepted. But
although this new and extended service worked most
profitably and satisfactorily to the government and the
public, the route between Suez and Bombay remained
under the control of the East India Company, notwithstanding the vessels employed by it were as slow and as
unsuitable to the service as those of the admiralty had
proved to be between England and Alexandria; and not-

withstanding, further, that the Peninsular and Oriental Company offered to perform the service in question for 17*s.* per mile in vessels of 500 horse-power, in place of service costing upwards of 30*s.* per mile in vessels of not half the power and of greatly inferior speed and accommodations. And it was not until 1854 that the Peninsular and Oriental Company could secure an additional contract for this service, and would not even then in all probability have got it, had not the great East India mail been lost about this time in the Indian Ocean while being transported in a sailing-craft.

Again : as their contracts on these different routes ran out, the government never in a single instance renewed them without throwing open the business to public competition, and continually imposing new and onerous conditions. In one instance, about 1852, when coal rose temporarily from 36*s.* to 60*s.* per ton, and the company, for lack of supply, found it difficult to carry out a portion of their service, the government threatened to inflict a penalty of £35,000 for its non-performance, and would have done so had not the company by strenuous efforts, and at great expense, met the emergency. In 1856, also, when the Peninsular and Oriental Company were unwilling on simply business grounds to comply with certain new conditions of service between Suez and Australia, the government at once took the business from them, and accepted the tender of another company, which afterwards failed most disastrously, and lost its entire capital.

Owing, however, to the long connection of this great steamship line with the government, and the large amounts of money paid it from time to time from the public treasury for its great and varied service, the idea has come to prevail, even in England, that the company was not only called into existence in the first instance by the government, but also has always been maintained by it. But on this point Mr. Lindsay, in his History of Merchant Shipping, speaks thus decisively : —

" The impression that this company owed its origin to government grants, and that it has been entirely maintained by subsidies for the conveyance of the mails, is not supported by facts. Indeed, during the earlier portions of its career the company, by agreeing to carry the Peninsular mails, shortly after it had been started, for a sum considerably less than the cost of maintaining the admiralty packets then employed, with a speed, too, and regularity previously unknown, conferred an undoubted boon on the public.

" Whether the company would have continued to maintain its career of prosperity without government subsidies, is a problem too speculative for me to solve. Free from the conditions required by the government, the company would probably have done better for its shareholders, had it been at liberty to build and sail its ships as it pleased, despatching them on such voyages and at such rates of speed as paid it best: and in support of this opinion I may remark, that various other shipping companies, with no assistance whatever from government, have yielded far larger dividends than the Peninsular and Oriental ; and, further, that private ship-owners who never had a mail-bag in their steamers have realized large fortunes."

And again, after reviewing the fiscal condition of the company, Mr. Lindsay continues, —

" From whatever cause it may have arisen, the fact is apparent, that, though the annual gross receipts of the company are enormous, its expenditure is so great that less balance is left for the shareholders than is usually divided among those of undertakings of a similar character which receive no assistance from government, but are free to employ their ships in whatever branch of commerce they can be most profitably engaged."

The evidence is therefore conclusive, that Great Britain has never done what it is proposed that the government of the United States shall do ; namely, directly appropriate large amounts of the public money for the sole and exclusive purpose of encouraging shipping. The extent and wide separation of her dependencies have required her to maintain a costly ocean mail-service, involving large payments to various steamship lines, which payments in turn have undoubtedly helped these lines, and in some instances have enabled them to run where otherwise they would not. But in every case these payments, by whatever name they be designated, have been no more than was indispensable to secure the necessary mail or other government service ; and no act of British legislation can be cited to show that money was ever voted by Parliament for the purpose of aiding in the construction and employment of ships for the British commercial marine. " And, if the British Government were to resolve to discontinue every possible patronage to its shipping, it could not reduce its payment to the extent of one pound, and for the reason that all that it pays is now absolutely necessary in order to get the required ocean mail-service." [1]

That these conclusions are also in accord with the views of the one witness who, above all others, by reason of his official position in the British Government and his recognized eminence as a statesman and economist, must be regarded as an authority, — namely, the Rt. Hon. Henry

---

[1] At a recent launching on the Clyde of one of the new ships of the Williams & Guion Line, Mr. Guion, one of the principal owners, after rehearsing the success of the company, remarked triumphantly that his corporation "had never received a penny of government subsidy, and felt no necessity of it."

At the annual meeting of the Peninsular and Oriental Steamship Company, held in London, Dec. 8, 1881, the chairman, referring to the connection of the company with the British Post-Office Department, also used the following language : —

"Referring to the financial aspect of the postal-service contracts, they had received £75,000 less from the present than from the late contract, while the service they had now to perform was far more arduous. At the expiration of the late contract a very serious attempt was made to wrest from them the position they had held as contractors for the Eastern mails for forty years. They had obtained the new contract, not through any favoritism, or because they had done the work so long, or on account of the great public services which they had rendered during their career, but simply because the service they had offered was the best, and the price they had asked was the lowest. It was sometimes said that a mail-service was very easy; but he assured them that the service they had to perform was very difficult, and he was not sure that it was profitable. He was, however, sure that they had had to build much more expensive vessels than the commercial character of their work required."

Fawcett, M.P., Professor of Political Economy in the University of Cambridge, Eng., and present (1882) British postmaster-general, — will be evident from the following extract from a recently (1881) published review by this gentleman of the effects of bounties on shipping : [1] —

"Before leaving the subject, it may be well to refer to the fact that such subsidies as these which have been considered are sometimes defended on the ground that England gives similar assistance to her shipping trade in the form of postal subsidies. It is, however, obvious that there is an essential difference between a postal subsidy and one given on the building of a ship. In the case of France it is admitted that the latter is granted to compensate French ship-builders for the extra price they have to pay for materials in consequence of the tariff. A postal subsidy, on the other hand, is simply a payment made for the conveyance, under certain specified conditions as to time and speed, of postal matter. Such a payment may raise many important questions of administration. Thus, on the one hand, it has been contended that the State does not receive a service which is equivalent to the amount paid; and that an equally good, if not an improved conveyance of the mails would be secured if they were treated more as ordinary merchandise. On the other hand, it has been urged, that, without some special arrangement being entered into, there are many cases in which regularity of conveyance would not be insured, and that this regularity is so important that the amount paid in the form of a postal subsidy to secure it represents a judicious outlay on the part of the State. Without expressing an opinion on the various questions which may thus be suggested, it is evident that they raise issues very different from those which are involved in a discussion as to the relative advantages of free trade and protection. And as a further proof that

---

[1] Free Trade and Protection. By Henry Fawcett, M.P. Fourth edition, 1881, pp. 29, 38. Macmillan & Co., London.

postal subsidies are not granted with the object of giving to English shipping any protection against the competition of the shipping of other countries, it may be mentioned that when a contract for the conveyance of mails is advertised, no restriction whatever is imposed upon any foreign vessels competing; and the subsidy would be paid to foreign owned and foreign built vessels if it were considered that the best and cheapest conveyance of mails would thus be secured. For some years a subsidy was paid by the English Post Office to a German steamship-company for the conveyance of mails from Southampton to New York."

Recent Experience of France.

The commercial marine of France, having, in common with that of the United States and Italy, lapsed into chronic decay, the French Government recently determined to unreservedly adopt the system of bounties or subsidies, with a view of restoring this department of its industries; and accordingly, by a law passed in January, 1881, it offered large premiums for the building and navigation of French vessels, both sail and steam. The matter was previously thoroughly discussed in the National Assembly and throughout the country; and there was no misconception on the part of the French public in respect to at least two points: *first*, that the proposition to offer bounties was in itself an acknowledgment of an inability on the part of France to compete with other maritime nations; and *second*, that, for the purpose of encouraging the French shipping interest, an extra tax of a considerable amount was to be imposed upon the country at large and upon all its other industries. And still another point, specially worthy of note by citizens of the United States in this connection, is, that the new French law did not propose, even at the outset, or embody in its enactment, any inhibition whatever on the citizens of France from buying ships in foreign countries, and making them French property, in case they desired to do so ; but, on the contrary, it offers a premium for so doing, by giving one-half the subsidy granted to French-built ships to vessels of foreign construction bought by citizens of France and transferred to the French flag.

As already stated, the French scheme of subventions relates both to the building and navigation of ships ; but very different reasons are assigned in the body of the law for the legislation in question in respect to these two classes of industrial transactions. Thus, in respect to ship-building, the act declares that the subsidies are granted to compensate ship-builders for the duties on im-ported materials entering into the construction of ships in France ; while the subsidies granted for the employment of vessels are asserted to be "for the purpose of com-pensating the mercantile navy for the service it renders the country in the recruitment of the military navy." [1]

---

[1] The French subsidies granted for ship-building are estimated upon the gross tonnage, and are as follows : For iron and steel vessels, 60 francs per ton; for wooden vessels of 200 tons or more, 20 francs per ton ; for wooden vessels less than 200 tons, 10 francs per ton; for composite vessels, 40 francs

The first effect of the law was to induce, with almost feverish haste, the formation of a number of new and extensive steamship companies ; and the construction of a number of new and large steamers was promptly commenced and rapidly pushed forward in various French ports, as well as in the shipyards of Great Britain.   But as all these enterprises are in effect guaranteed against loss by the government, and as any business they may do is so much gain, they are of necessity essentially speculative in character.   And that they are so regarded by the capitalists that have embarked in them, is made evident by the business they propose to do ; one line, for example, having been formed to trade between Havre and the Southern Seas, and another to run on a long circuitous voyage between France, Quebec, Halifax, St. Thomas, and Brazil.

The results of the first year's experience of this French system, so far as reported, have not proved satisfactory.

---

per ton ; for engines placed on board steamers, and for auxiliary apparatus, boilers, pipes, etc., 12 francs per 100 kilograms.

The navigation bounty is fixed at 1 franc 50 centimes per registered ton per 1,000 miles run for new vessels. It is confined to vessels engaged in foreign trade, and is to be reduced annually during a period of ten years, when it will cease. For foreign-built vessels the bounty is reduced one-half of the above assigned amounts. Vessels taking out French registers before the promulgation of this law are to be regarded as vessels of French construction. The navigation bounty is increased 15 per cent in the case of vessels built according to plans approved by the French Marine Department. Vessels receiving bounties are required to carry the French mails and post-office agents free of charge.

Bounties were granted for the encouragement of voyages between French ports, the French colonies, and countries out of Europe; but the returns for 1881 show a very marked decrease in the French tonnage engaged in her colonial trade as compared with 1880, when there were no bounties; while the French tonnage entries into French ports from foreign countries showed a decrease in 1881 as compared with 1880, with some marked gain in the same time in respect to clearances. But what is most noticeable is, that the entries and clearances of foreign tonnage (which of course receives no bounty) into French ports during 1881 showed a very large increase as compared with 1880, and was apparently in no ways affected by the new and discriminating privileges extended to French shipping in order to enable it to successfully compete for foreign business.

Recent Experience of Germany.

Impressed, and apparently favorably, with the plan adopted by the French Government for the encouragement of its merchant shipping, the German Government, under the auspices of Prince Bismarck, submitted during the past year (1881) an exhibit of the French law to the Reichstag, and accompanied it with the question, " if it was not worthy the serious consideration of that body, whether under the present circumstances German navigation and trade will be able to thrive and to compete with those of other nations aided by state subsidies?" Thus

far the " Reichstag " has taken no action on the subject ;
but the proposal to meet French subsidies to French shipping with German subsidies to German shipping promptly
called out most energetic protests from the **merchants of
not only the** old Hanse towns of **Hamburg and** Bremen,
but also from all the other German seaports on the Baltic
and North Seas, with, it is stated, the simple exception of
the small and almost insignificant port of Papenburg, in
the Duchy of Oldenburg. And, **as a** specimen of these
protests, **the following translation of that of the** " Hamburg Respectable **Merchants'** Society " (" *der ehrbare
Kaufmann* ") is submitted : —

"Thus far," after a formal preliminary, it says, "German commerce and navigation have been **able** to compete with those of other
nations, and their present **strong** position is chiefly due **to** their own
exertions. Even if the French Government should extend larger
monopolies and subsidies to their national trade and commerce, the
Hamburg shipping merchants are not afraid, that, if let alone, their
own development would be injured or suffer under such adverse legislation. The growth and prosperity of national trade are, before all,
created by the natural talent and disposition of a people. Governmental measures, whether they consist in throwing artificial obstacles
in the way of foreign competition or in direct support of the national
flag, may here and there bring temporary advantages to individual
enterprises ; but they will never be able permanently to raise and ele-
vate the shipping interest. On the contrary, as experience has shown
in France, they paralyze individual energy, and endanger the spirit of
enterprise, and effect the decline, if not the ruin, of trade. In the
interest of German commerce and of the national flag, the Hamburg
merchants most earnestly and respectfully pray that all governmental
measures for their protection be definitively set aside."

The German Government at present contributes nothing in the way of aid to her commercial marine, but pays for postal freight forwarded by her steamers about 200,000 marks per annum. Nevertheless the German shipping interests — represented especially by a splendid fleet of merchant steamships built mainly in Great Britain — are most prosperous; although Germany by situation and traditions can hardly be regarded as a maritime nation. Italy, with a decaying marine, is reported as paying annually $1,500,000 as a contribution for her steamship service. The annual payments of Austria for the same object are reported at $500,000, while in the case of Belgium and Holland the contributions are very inconsiderable.

A Repeal of our Navigation Laws not alone Sufficient to Arrest the Decadence of American Shipping.

We come, finally, to the third objection made to the repeal of the navigation laws; namely, that the repeal would not effect the end desired, or the restoration of the American shipping interest. In this objection, it must be admitted, there is much of validity. For, apart from the restrictions involved in our navigation code, the ownership and use of ships has been clogged and burdened with so many other onerous conditions in the United States, that, were the right to purchase and use ships of foreign construction at once fully and freely conceded to our citizens, their successful employment in competition with vessels under foreign flags engaged in foreign trade would be not

a little difficult, if not altogether impossible. Nevertheless, the repeal of our navigation laws is the first step to
be taken ; and, in default of this, nothing practical can be
done for the relief of our American shipping.   So long as
our ship-builders are effectually shielded from the effects
of foreign competition, they will never, we may be sure,
build ships at the lowest possible cost.   It is but human
nature for them not to do it.   With the navigation laws
repealed, some ships will at once be purchased and put
into profitable use.   One of the Southern railroads,
adapted for the carrying of cotton from the interior to a
seaboard port, some time since, would very gladly have
put on a line of freight (cotton) steamers from their termi-
nus to New York, if the proper ships could be obtained at
a satisfactory cost.   Such ships cannot now be had in the
United States ; but the company can procure them exceedingly cheap, because of old but desirable pattern for the
business in question, in England.   But, as foreign-built
ships cannot participate in the coasting trade, the project necessarily had to be abandoned, and with it the development of a new local Southern industry.   When the
Chinese ports and inland navigation were first opened to
foreigners, American capital and enterprise at once introduced light and fleet steamers of the American pattern to
do the business before transacted by the slow and unwieldy
junks, and for a time held almost the monopoly of transportation for freights and passengers on certain routes.
As the steamers, however, wore out, it became desirable

to replace them with English-built iron steamers of improved pattern ; but as such steamers could not fly the American flag, or be entitled to protection from the American diplomatic and consular representatives in China, or fly the British flag without passing under British control, and as the Chinese flag and protection were not desirable, a large and profitable business established by Americans was gradually abandoned, and permitted to pass into the hands of the representatives of other nationalities. But, had there been no home navigation code to prevent, the American flag would doubtless now be most prominent on the Chinese coast and inland waters, and large profits would have accrued to American seamen and capitalists.[1]

Repeal, then, our navigation laws, and abandon both the idea and the proposition to reward men by grants of money for building the dearest ships in the world, and a leverage is at once gained for the removal of other obstacles and abuses.

Without repeal, the decay of our merchant marine will continue from bad to worse, until within a very few years our flag will substantially vanish from the ocean. With

---

[1] Of the tonnage employed in coast and river trade between the treaty ports of China, 40 per cent was reported as once bearing the flag of the United States. At present this trade is nearly equally divided between British and Chinese bottoms ; and, according to a recent consular report to the State Department at Washington, there is now but one small steamer upon the whole coast of Eastern Asia that carries our flag.

repeal, we shall be encouraged to greater efforts, and shall at least have sufficient of hope given us for the future to warrant our continuing to use the anchor as one of the emblems of American industry.

To the nature of these further obstacles it is next proposed to ask attention.

CHAPTER IX.

OBSTACLES IN THE WAY OF THE RESTORATION OF THE MERCHANT MARINE OF THE UNITED STATES, OTHER THAN OUR NAVIGATION LAWS.

As already stated, it would be an error to suppose that a repeal of our navigation laws will at once and alone re-create our commercial marine. The repeal is the first step to be taken. It is the indispensable step. It will be the beginning of a new era of prosperity for our shipping interests. But through long public indifference to this subject, through actual hostility to ships and foreign commerce (as will be hereafter proved), through the habit of disregarding the results of thorough economic investigations, and styling the men who make them as theorists and unpractical, and the man of business, who in nine cases out of ten works in a limited sphere, knows little beyond that sphere, and rarely stops to study, investigate, or generalize, as the practical one whose advice and counsel is always to have the preference, — through all these agencies there has been created a series of other obstacles in the way of the profitable employment of American vessels in foreign commerce, so serious and destructive, that if ships of the best foreign construction were to-day put down at our wharves as free gifts, their use in competition with vessels under foreign flags would be attended with not a little of embarrassment, if not wholly impracticable.

The Obstacle of Local Taxation.

The most serious of these obstacles grows out of the system of State or local taxation generally adopted in the several States in the Federal Union ; and which, starting with the theory that in order to tax equitably it is necessary to tax every thing, includes in the assessment lists real and personal property, things tangible and intangible, the visible, corporeal substance, the product of labor, and the invisible, incorporeal title, which only represents, and is not itself the product of labor any more than a shadow is the substance. Under such system, the like of which does not exist in any other country on the face of the globe, and which of necessity breaks down in application because the law cannot provide clairvoyant assessors, gifted to see what cannot be seen and to touch what is not tangible, ships are taxed as personal property to their owners.

The manner now in which local taxes work to the disadvantage of American shipping and commercial interests may be thus illustrated : Let us suppose the projection of a new line of steamships to run between the United States and Europe in competition with existing lines, now controlled by foreign capitalists and registered under a foreign flag. If the nationality of the company is to be American, and its location any one of our leading Atlantic cities, — except Philadelphia, — the taxation, until within the past year, on the whole capital or property of the company — ships, wharves, machine-shops, offices, and floating capital — would have been from 1.50 to 2.50, or even greater per cent, on a pretty full valuation.[1]

Furthermore, until recently, the National Government would have preferred an average tax under the tariff of about forty per cent on all articles of foreign production entering into the construction of vessels ; and, as a consequence, it advanced the price of similar articles of domestic production to an equal or nearly corresponding extent. **By the Act of June,** 1872, however, articles of

---

[1] The State of Pennsylvania, when she, some years ago, incorporated a local transatlantic steamship company having its *situs* in Philadelphia, judiciously exempted all ships engaged in foreign trade, as well as all other property — stocks, bonds, etc. — of the company in question, from all State taxation; and, during the year 1881, the States of New York and Massachusetts also exempted ships owned by their citizens, and engaged in foreign trade, from all direct State taxation. In all, or nearly all, of the other States, the taxation of vessels, whether engaged in foreign trade or otherwise, is, however, still maintained; and the following illustration of its working in Illinois, and on the shipping of the Lakes, has recently been brought forward in Chicago. Thus a wooden sailing-vessel, it is stated, built to carry grain through the Welland Canal, costs about twenty thousand dollars. This vessel, if owned in Chicago, would be assessed by the local authorities at ten thousand dollars; and at the rate of five per cent — State and city tax rate for 1880 — the amount chargeable would be five hundred dollars. The same vessel, if owned in Canada, would not pay any thing directly, nor in Liverpool apart from an income tax on the profits of the owners individually.

foreign growth or production, "necessary for the construction and equipment of vessels built in the United States for the purpose of being engaged in foreign trade," may be imported in bond free of duty ; but vessels receiving the benefit of this provision are not allowed to engage in the coastwise trade of the United States for more than two months in any one year. As one consequence of this restriction, a New York ship-owner stated at the meeting of the National Board of Trade in December, 1880, that, having occasion to send a vessel built for foreign trade from New York to New Orleans for temporary employment, he was obliged, before he could do it, to pay four hundred dollars for duties on the suit of metal which had been previously placed on the ship's bottom ; or he was, in fact, fined to this extent for using his own property in a perfectly honest but not lawful industry.

For some years after the war, also, when the shipping interest of the United States engaged in foreign trade had suffered exceptionally from the inability of the Government to protect it from Confederate cruisers, and when it therefore needed the kindliest and most fostering care, income taxes were imposed on the incomes of ship-owners (if they perchance happened to have any), and, in addition, heavy taxes on the gross receipts of their entire business, and upon every passenger ticket by them sold. When the largest possible damage had been effected, these national taxes were repealed. But the practice of Great Britain and other nations of allowing vessels employed in

foreign commerce to take stores for voyage consumption
out of bond, free of duty, has not as yet been thought
worthy of imitation ; and, as a consequence, the cost of
ship-supplies in the United States was reported by a committee of Congress a few years ago to be about twenty per
cent in the aggregate in excess of the cost of supplies to
vessels of Great Britain.

If now, on the other hand, the *situs* of the prospective
new steamship company is made foreign, and its location
fixed at Liverpool, the whole amount of local taxation to
which the company would be subjected would be merely
an assessment to the extent of from ten to twenty-five per
cent on the rental — not capital — value of the premises
occupied either as offices, storehouses, or machine-shops.
Beyond this the British Government would levy an income-
tax on the profits (if any) of the shareholders or owners,
as individuals, to the extent of from one to two per cent,
and, omitting all other forms of direct taxation, would allow
all articles subject to taxation, either under the excise or
tariff, such as distilled spirits, teas, coffee, wines, and
tobacco, which may be required for use on board the
steamer in question, to be taken from bond free of duty.
The difference in the return on the investment, therefore,
growing out of the difference merely in the fiscal systems
recognized in the different locations specified, would be
of itself sufficient to afford to the foreign capitalist a
dividend on his stock equal to at least one-half of the
ordinary rate of European interest on the capital em-

ployed; while to the American investor the disadvantage would have at least an expression twofold greater through an increase of expenses and a diminution of profit which can be traced directly to a system of taxation which has enhanced the price of every thing that has entered into the steamer, from the laying of her keel to the coal that feeds her engines. In Great Britain and other countries it is furthermore to be noted that the ownership of a ship that is idle and not earning, or employed and not earning, does not entail any burden of taxation; but in the United States it makes no difference whether the ship be at work or idle, profitably or unprofitably employed, she pays taxes all the same.[1]

With competition with foreign nations on terms of equality being, therefore, from the very outset, not less by State than by Federal laws, rendered impossible, is it to be wondered at that the American ocean marine has

---

[1] The above illustration of the difference of taxation in the case of domestic and foreign steamships was first presented to the public by the writer in a report to the Legislature of New York on local taxation in 1871, and has since been used by him in other essays on the same subject. No one questioned then, or has questioned since, the accuracy of the statements; and yet, until within a very recent period, the presentation of the above embodied facts has produced no more effect on legislative assemblies — National or State — than if the same number of words had been written in Sanscrit. Boards of trade, commercial conventions, and legislative assemblies continued, however, to pass resolutions all the same, deploring the decay of American shipping, and recommending a liberal grant of subsidies to set matters right again, and doubtless considered their duties discharged in expressing their sentiments.

declined almost to extinction, or that there are so few mechanical establishments in the United States capable of building or repairing first-class steamships?

As, however, to some minds, the fact that foreign countries exempt their shipping from all direct taxation as property, may not seem conclusive in favor of allowing a similar exemption of similar property in the United States, it may be well at this point to ask attention to what may be termed the common-sense theory of taxation. Thus, taxes, it must be admitted, are the consideration which persons and property pay for the protection of the State; for unless life, liberty, and property are made reasonably secure, production will not go forward. The soldier or policeman guards while the laborer or artisan performs his labor in safety. The State is always, therefore, an important partner in all production; and in every equitable system of taxation the taxes paid will form a part of the cost of all production, and enter into and constitute a part of the market value of all products. If, now, the State does not give to the citizen the protection he needs in return for his taxes, the levy which the State makes upon the property of the citizen is not entitled to be called taxation, but is spoliation, plunder, or the arbitrary taking of property without compensation. Everybody can see this, if the citizen after paying for policemen is robbed with impunity; if, after paying for courts and congresses to make and administer just laws, he is deprived of lawful liberty; if, after paying for an army and navy, he is made needlessly subject to inroads from foreign foes. But people do not so readily see that the same principle of spoliation is involved when the State allows untaxed property to be brought into free competition and use with property of the same description and use which it has caused to be burdened with taxes. What sort of competition would there be, for example, in the dry-goods trade, if Chicago assessed a rate of 5 per cent, or New York City one of 2.3 per cent, on all the dry-goods stores bearing even street-numbers, and entirely exempted from all taxation all the corresponding stores bearing uneven numbers? The merchants of the first class would be crushed: there would be a popular outcry against so manifest an injustice, and the courts would promptly compel the assessors to do equity. And yet the personal tax on resident owners of ships in various States of the Federal Union, while there is freedom from taxation of competing ships engaged in the same foreign trade but owned in Montreal, England, France, and other countries, where ships are untaxed, is no different. In the one case it is not a tax on the dry-goods business, and the other it is not a tax on ships, but an arbitrary spoliation of the even-numbered merchant and the resident ship-owner. In this light, does it not, we ask, seem incredible that a tax so unjust and offensive should exist in the nineteenth century, or be enforced against respectable ship-owners, guilty of no crime, — unless residence is such, — and entitled in justice to the protection of the law?

Obstruction of Tonnage-Taxes, Consular Fees, Pilot-Charges, etc.

Tonnage-taxes on shipping are not levied by **Great** Britain, nor, it is believed, by any other of the maritime states of Europe, except Spain. Prior to the war, also, there were no tonnage-taxes in the United States; and their enactment in 1862 was due simply and exclusively to the urgent necessities of the government for revenue occasioned by the war. Those necessities having long since passed, **there** is no good or sufficient reason for the continuance of such taxes. The rates imposed on American and foreign vessels being substantially the same, American vessels would **not** seem to **be** relatively at **a** disadvantage with foreign vessels on account **of** these taxes. But really they are; inasmuch as in the one case the effect of the tax is generally to reduce realized profits, while in the other it constitutes, under existing circumstances, an obstacle, as will be presently shown, in the way of realizing any profits at all.

According to British maritime rules, the tonnage capacity of vessels is reckoned on only such space as is available for cargo; and in the measurement of vessels for the ascertainment **of** their capacity, allowance is made for the space occupied for the accommodation of the officers and crew and also by the machinery. In the United States the space occupied by the water-closets and galley are **alone exempted from** admeasurement; and as a consequence, American vessels are **at a** disadvantage **as** compared with British shipping in respect **to** tonnage and **harbor dues and light-money** in ports where such taxes are levied. Moreover, a sailing-vessel which enters an American port once a year is obliged **to** pay as much tonnage-tax as a steamer that enters the same port every month ; and if in a given line a steamer which has paid her tonnage-taxes for a year becomes disabled, and is withdrawn during the first month of the year, the substitute steamer must pay tonnage all the same for another full year.

The charges of our consular system are claimed to be another weighty burden on American shipping engaged in foreign trade.[1] These fees are all fixed by Congress, are paid into the United States Treasury, and have evidently been arranged with the idea of not only rendering the United States consular system self-sustaining, but of also making it (as it actually is) a source of national revenue. Now, so long as the Federal Government was in urgent **need of** revenue, the policy of making our consular system self-supporting was defensible ; but with an annual revenue so far in excess of the needs of the government that the disposal of the surplus is a source of difficulty **and** a temptation to waste and extravagance, the continued levy of special taxes, in the form of excessive and un-

---

[1] By **virtue** of a provision attached to an appropriation bill passed by Congress in 1880, the consular fees of the United States were made conformable to the standard adopted by Great Britain.

necessary consular fees, on an interest so unfortunate and depressed as American shipping, is without justification.

Again, under the present United States system of appointing consuls for political reasons mainly, and with a knowledge on the part of these officials that their term of office is always uncertain and generally short, there is little inducement for good and intelligent service; and, as a rule, every construction of law unfavorable to the ship-owner, and advantageous to the consul or the government, is taken advantage of, and generally submitted to by the victims, as involving less expense and trouble than the seeking and obtaining of redress through an appeal to the State Department at Washington. On the other hand, the British consul is certain of his position during good behavior and competency; and he also knows that he stands in direct line of promotion under the civil-service system of his country. The consequence is, that Great Britain has a host of faithful and experienced consuls, men who feel the importance of looking out for the interests of their own commerce, and do so both from a sense of duty and a sense of patriotism.

Compulsory **pilotage, the three** months' extra pay to crews discharged in foreign lands, and the obligatory employment of government officials for the shipment of sailors in American ports, are all barnacles also which impede the progress of our commercial marine, and require to be speedily scraped off as a pre-requisite to its full **development.**

By a system of compulsory dues on incoming and out going vessels (from which only the coasting service is exempt) the Sandy Hook pilot-service of the port of New York, which consists of 133 New York and 58 New Jersey pilots, derives a yearly income from the commerce of that port of $800,000 to $1,000,000. The specific amounts charged are said to be two and a half times in excess of what is paid in Liverpool for similar service; and at the Shipping Convention at Boston in October, 1880, Mr. James E. Ward of New York stated that his firm "paid as large an amount for pilotage into New York Harbor as they did to the captain of his steamship for sailing the vessel all the way to Cuba and back, facing all the dangers of the seas and the risk of contagion in Cuba." These compulsory pilot-charges contribute to make New York one of the most expensive ports for shipping in the world; and it does not look hopeful for the consummation of any plans for the restoration of our shipping when it is remembered, that although the merchants of New York have for years petitioned the Legislature on the subject, and have presented their case in the most conclusive manner, they have not yet been able to obtain any redress for this grievance.

The complaint of the so-called "Three Months' Wages Law" is founded upon a Federal statute enacted as far back as 1803, when there was comparatively little communication between the United States and various foreign countries; and which provides, that, whenever a sailor is discharged from an American vessel in a foreign port, he shall be paid three months' **extra wages.** The **original intent** of this law was good, and was to **prevent seamen from** being left alone and destitute in a strange port ; but now, when vessels are constantly going into and coming out of every civilized port in the world, and the great mass of sailors, being of foreign nationality, are as much **at** home at one port as another, there is no longer any necessity for its continuance, inasmuch as there is no danger that any able-bodied seaman will ever lack opportunities for employment in any port at any time. Under existing circumstances the law subserves little other purpose than to furnish a never-ending source of dispute and bad temper between captains, crews, **and** consular **officers,** and ought to be repealed.

In addition to the burdens and grievances above noticed, to which the merchant marine of **the** United States is subjected, there has also grown up, under our national policy of ignorance and neglect, a host of other petty and vexatious taxes on shipping, the nature of which **can be** best illustrated by recounting the experience **of a vessel** entering or clearing from **the port of New York, the** point where in 1880 nearly 57 per cent of the entire foreign commerce of the country was concentrated.

After the **pilot,** whose charges range from $3.70 per foot for vessels drawing 13 **feet of** water, to $6.50 per foot for vessels in excess of 20 feet draught, comes the health-officer, whose fee for inspection, and permit to proceed

into port, is $6.50 for sailing-vessels. The "boarding-offi-
cer," a custom-house inspector, is the next to board the
vessel; but for his services no charge is made. Then
comes the harbor-master; and under State laws he is allowed a fee of 1½ cents per ton on the tonnage of each
vessel, — a rate which varies in the ports of the different
States. Then every sailing-master is required to go to
the custom-house as soon as his vessel arrives, and pay
certain charges and small fees. Both foreign and American vessels must pay $3.17 fee when their cargoes are not
dutiable, and $5.50 when the cargoes are dutiable. The
amount returned for the year 1881, as collected under the
head of customs-officers' fees and services, was $720,265.
Vessels in excess of 100 tons burden pay a tonnage-tax
once a year at the rate of 30 cents per ton; and the amount
collected under this head for 1881 was about $280,000.
Each American vessel in addition is also required to pay
hospital dues of 40 cents per month per man, payments
to be made each time that a vessel enters. These dues
are for the support of the marine-hospital service of the
United States, and the total collections for this purpose
for the year 1881 were returned at $380,518. Before the
war, the marine-hospital tax was only 20 cents per month.
In the Dominion of Canada, the equivalent tax is only
two cents per ton, payable once a year on vessels under
100 tons, and three times a year on vessels over that
tonnage. Should the owner or master of any incoming
vessel desire to secure special permits from the custom-

house for different purposes, he may do so by paying
20 cents extra for each paper. Frequently a single vessel
will require half a dozen of these permits. A wharfage
tax, imposed by the State, is two cents per ton for the
first 200 tons, and one-fourth of a cent for each additional
ton per day. Then come the expenses of towing backward and forward, port-warden's fees, bills for unloading,
etc.; and by the time that the ship-owner has disposed of
his cargo, and settled up for the trip, he finds that a good
share of his revenues from the voyage has been paid out
in compulsory fees and expenses.[1]

Outgoing vessels from New York experience also almost as much inconvenience and expense in "getting
away" from port as do incoming vessels in "getting in"
to port. "When the master of a vessel is arranging for a

---

[1] The following exhibit, copied from the columns of "The New York
Times," shows in detail what it cost a bark of 654 tons, arriving from
Manilla in the spring of 1882, to secure a landing in New York City:—

For pilotage	$80 50
Health-officer's fee	6 50
Entry fee at custom-house	5 50
Permits, extra	40
United States Hospital money	64 00
Harbor-master's charges	9 80
Wharfage fees	5 13
Tonnage-duty, 30 cents per ton, 654 tons	196 20
Total	$368 03

With an increase in the size of the ship, the expenses as above enumerated will of course also increase.

voyage, it becomes necessary for him to ship his crew.   If
he intends going to any other than the West Indies,
Gulf, or Nova Scotia ports, he is obliged to appear before
a United States shipping commissioner, and ship his
entire crew under the supervision of that officer, paying
$2 per man for so doing.   The law requires that each and
every seaman about to sail for any ports, except those
mentioned above, must appear before the United States
commissioner, sober, and sign the articles there.   In addition to the fee of $2 per man, the sailing-master must
obtain from the commissioner a blank for the official log,
two blanks for the ship's articles, and two blanks for
copies of the crew-list   The cost of these blanks is about
$3.   After arranging every thing pertaining to the crew,
the sailing-master must proceed to the custom-house, and
obtain his clearance papers.   For an American vessel
bound for a foreign port, the cost of these papers is $3.25.
Then come the fees for outward-bound pilotage, which
are about the same as for incoming vessels."

For vessels engaged in the coasting trade, there is a
different system of fees and charges ; and these, it was
recently stated (March 8, 1882) by Hon. W. H. Frye,
United States Senator from Maine, have increased "at
least ten times, within the last twenty years." [1]   In illus-

---

[1] " The old fee for measuring was 50 cents a ton for a vessel of 5 tons
and less than 20.   If 20 tons and not over 70, it was 75 cents ; if 70 tons and
not over 100, $1 ; and if over 100 tons, it was $1.50 : and yet ' The Louise A.
Boardman,' under your laws imposed since the war, was compelled to pay

tration in detail of these charges, the same senator detailed the following recent experience of an American coasting vessel : —

"Here is a coaster of 112 tons, 'The Louise A. Boardman:' she wants to sail from one of our ports to Calais, Me., and then across the river a quarter of a mile to St. Stephen's in the Provinces. We have quite a large trade with the Dominion of Canada, in which our vessels are engaged, as their vessels are engaged in sailing from their ports to ours. Now, what is that 'Louise A. Boardman' compelled under our law to pay? First: new vessel 112 tons, enrolment and bond, $1.10; license, $1.20; admeasurement, $15, — making $17.30. For clearance: register and bond, $2.25; certified list of crew and bond, 65 cents; certified shipping-papers, 20 cents; entry, $2.50; blanks, 40 cents, — making $6 more. Then for entry: entry, $2.50; hospital money, five men, one month, $2. A little schooner of 112 tons paying $24 a year hospital tax, while the English tax is only two cents a month, and they have as good hospitals as we do! Tonnage, 112 tons at 30 cents a ton, making this little schooner pay $33.60, if she happens to go from Calais across to St. Stephen's. That was nothing but a war-tax, never imposed before the war; and still Congress permits it to be kept on these coasting vessels. Further: for permit to land, 20 cents; protections, 20 cents; bill of health, with report, 20 cents; blanks, 10 cents, — making in all $38.80. Again, charge to enrolment and license: enrolment and bond, $1.10; license, $1.20, — making $2.30. That American schooner of 112 tons burden is obliged to pay under our laws all those immense and bur-

---

$15 for that admeasurement instead of $1.50. For enrolment under the old law (before the war), 50 cents; now $2.25. For license under the old law 25 cents not over 20 tons, 50 cents where the vessel is 100 tons and not under 20, over 100 tons $1." — *Speech of W. H. Frye, United States Senator, Congressional Record, March* 8, 1882.

densome taxes; and the attention of Congress has been called to it
again and again, and yet no relief has been offered."

"What does 'The Louise A. Boardman' have to pay if she gets
out papers over in St. Stephen's instead of Calais? She would be
compelled to pay two cents a month for a hospital tax per man, and
$2 for admeasurement, and no other namable tax whatever. Where a
schooner made ten or twelve voyages from our ports to Canadian
ports in a year, I have known her under our law to be compelled to
pay one-tenth of her whole value for United States taxes." — *Congressional Record, March 8, 1882.*

From the above statements, it appears that what may
be termed the "port" or "local" taxes and charges on
American shipping are excessive, vexatious, and for the
most part unnecessary, and in excess of the corresponding charges of other countries. Nearly all of them were
greatly increased during the war period, and have not
since been reduced in common with other similar taxes
on domestic industries and products. It should be also
specially noted, that the Federal Government imposes no
such taxes and restrictions on any other species of property or other branches of domestic industry as it does on
ships, and the owning and employment of ships, with the
exception of the manufacture and sale of distilled spirits
and tobacco, under the internal revenue system; and these
exceptions exist simply because the obtaining of revenue
from them is considered necessary and expedient, —
reasons which do not apply to ships and shipping.

An Illustration from Real Life and Experience.

How the situation operates to crush out all spirit of enterprise, and to discourage that practical, intelligent **class** of Americans, who, following the example of their fathers and the traditions of their country, invest their **little** capital or earnings in ships, and, personally superintending what they invest, try to make a living from the "abundance of the seas" as navigators rather than as merchants, may perhaps be better illustrated by the following incident of real life rather than by any abstract statements : In 1877 the writer was one of a commission appointed by the authorities of the State of New York to consider and report on the subject of the tolls, the revenues, and the commerce of the canals of the State; and, as a part of the investigation which was instituted in connection with the same, frequent visits were made in the month of December to the fleet of canal-boats, which at that season of the year lay up for the winter by the acre at certain piers of the East River in the city of New York, for the purpose of conference with the men whose lives are spent on the canals, owning their boats in many instances, and living upon them continuously, with their families, all the year round. As he was leaving a pier near Coenties slip one day, he was accosted by an intelligent, typical-looking sailor as one could wish to see, who respectfully requested an interview. Other engagements being, however, pressing, and the stranger confessing to a lack of all information respecting the canals, the interview was avoided. But on a subsequent day the writer found himself, as he was again leaving the pier, again confronted by the same person, when the following conversation ensued : —

"Come, now, you must let me talk to you a little to-day. I know who you are. I belong up in your State of Connecticut, and I feel as though I had a right to consult you." — "Well, my friend," I replied, "what do you want to talk about?" — "I want to talk about my business, which is about as bad as it can be." — "What is your business?" — "I am the captain and a third owner of that vessel," pointing at the same time to a neat two-masted schooner of three hundred tons burden, which lay on one side of the wharf ; "and I run regularly — that is, if I can get a cargo — between New York and ——," naming a port in Florida.   "Won't you go aboard for a few minutes?"

Before accepting the invitation, I took a glance at the surroundings ; and the contrast, in respect to what was going on at the opposite sides of the pier, was most striking.   Right across from the American vessel lay a large three-masted ship or bark, flying the Bremen flag, and taking in a cargo for Rio.   Here every thing was life and animation.   Carts and drays, loaded and unloaded, coming and going, formed an almost continuous procession.   The cargo, consisting of flour, provisions, turpentine, rosin, and cases apparently of machinery and railroad equipments, was being hoisted in at both bow and stern, and preparations were evidently making also for the reception of a deck-load of lumber ; but, on the other side, where the American vessel was moored, every thing was dull and lifeless. Taking in the situation, I said to my new friend, "Before going on board your vessel, tell me the explanation of all this. How happens it that you do not appear to be doing any thing, while right opposite there is evidently plenty of business, and of business in a hurry?"— "Oh!" said he, "you do not want any explanation. You understand it well enough."— "Perhaps I do," I rejoined ; "but I would like to have your explanation."— "Well, then, that chap over there gets his vessel and all his equipments, to commence with, at from one-third to one-half less than I would have to pay for the same thing. Then, he can have all his stores free of duty. Nobody troubles him about what sort of a crew he shall have. He pays considerably less than I do ; but two of such men as I can get are worth three of his any day. And there is another thing, which is not much talked about, but it comes mighty hard. That fellow, I understand, doesn't pay any thing in the way of taxes where he belongs : but I belong up in Connecticut ; and my vessel was licensed at [naming a port on Connecticut River], and last year they charged me almost two per cent on pretty near my full value. But I tell you what I think is the meanest thing of all. Last spring I got a chance to charter for Rio, — just where that feller over there is going ; and before I could start I had to walk up to the custom-house and pay ninety dollars, cash down, for the privilege, which is almost six per cent on all we earned last year, and made us feel so poor that we didn't insure this year, and if any thing happens to the craft it's a dead loss." — "Taxed you ninety dollars!" I replied, with a feeling of some surprise : "I don't quite see into it." — "Well, come aboard and see the documents, and they will explain it." And going aboard, I found every thing as attractive inside as out, — the wife, a comely, intelligent, and modest woman, in the cabin, competent, as the husband said, to take her trick at the wheel, or make a reckoning ; a little daughter, in addition, who was setting the table for dinner ; and, in a recess of the cabin, a desk, from which were produced the papers that explained the ninety dollars specific taxation. It seems the schooner, having been engaged in the coasting trade, was only enrolled or licensed, and, as such, was not liable to the United States tonnage-tax ; but, as a condition of going to Rio, — i.e., engaging in foreign trade, — was required to be registered, and pay a tonnage-tax on so doing of thirty cents per ton, or ninety dollars in the aggregate ; and as the captain showed his register and receipt, and put his finger on the evidence of his payment, he said, somewhat emphatically, "Considering how rich Uncle Sam has got to be, and how poor our business is, I think this is a —— poor place for him to fish for revenue." — "But," said I, "as you seem to fully understand the situation, why do you not talk to your members of Congress as you have talked to me? Why do not you and some of your friends go to Washington, and plead your own cause?" — "Oh! that would be no use. We haven't time **or money to spare**; and they wouldn't pay any attention to us at Washington if we went there. No: I tell my wife and partners that we had better sell out next spring, and go at something else."

Here, then, is the whole case in respect to the situation and the decline in American shipping, as it were, in a nutshell; embodied in this simple, pathetic story of a representative of a class of American citizens who feel that their government **denies to** them the protection which it gives unsparingly to others, treats them with discriminating injustice, and is actually, year by year, crowding them out of a branch of national and legitimate industry. **As** the man whose load of ashes, in going up hill, had all dribbled out at the end of his cart, said to the boys who had followed him up and expected to be edified with certain pungent and profane remarks, "I sha'n't swear. I couldn't begin to do justice to the subject."

Reference has been made to the circumstance, that the merchant marine of Italy, alone of the States of Europe, is in a state of marked decadence, analogous to that which characterizes the merchant marine of the United States; and investigations recently conducted by the Italian Chambers show that the agencies which have mainly contributed to such a result in the former country **are** essentially **the same** as have been influential to the

same end in the latter, **namely,** unwise and excessive tax-
ation. Thus, for example, an **Italian** ship is subjected
to the following taxes : anchorage dues, sanitary dues,
consular dues ; registry and stamp taxes, which are not
defined, but are numerous **and onerous ; a** property-tax
which is calculated at 13.20 per cent on the annual revenue **reduced by** two-eighths ; contributions to a pension-
fund, which may be estimated at 200 francs ($40) per
annum, but which depends on the number of the crew ;
a tax on insurance at the rate of $2\frac{1}{2}$ per cent on the
premiums ; and, **finally, a** considerable **number of** minor
charges, as for "transcription of acts," "inspections,"
quay dues, etc., — all of which have either nothing corresponding in the charges of other European states, or
are comparatively much greater. Italy, however, can
offer one plea in justification of its policy which is not
available to the **United** States : namely, that its finances
are in such a condition that it is obliged to **resort to** every
expedient in the way of taxation in order to obtain rev-
enue sufficient to meet its expenditures. Another cause
that has also greatly contributed to the decline of Italian
shipping **is, that the country has** tenaciously clung to **its**
sailing-vessels, **and either through** lack of enterprise or
capital has been **slow to avail itself** of the economies of
steam, and of necessity, therefore, has lost ground in
competing with other **countries.** Its laws, however, place
no restraint on the purchase or use by its citizens of
vessels of foreign construction.

CHAPTER X.

THE FUNDAMENTAL **CAUSE OF THE** DECAY, **AND THE** PRESENT MAIN OBSTACLE **IN WAY** OF THE RESUSCI- TATION OF THE MERCHANT **MARINE** OF THE UNITED STATES.

FROM the **review of** the subject under consideration which has now been made, it would seem as **if** every thing possible had been **done to** discourage and prevent the ownership and **use** of ships for the purposes of ocean trade and transport by citizens of the United States. But there is something worse and more singular than any thing that has been heretofore related. There is a large and most influential class of persons in the United States who do not want ships, do not believe in their utility, or in the trade and commerce of which **they are** the necessary adjuncts and instrumentalities, and though restrained through fear of public opinion, in a great degree, from working openly, yet never fail, while professing to the contrary, **to do** all in their **power to** make **the** resusci- tation of American shipping impossible. And, thus far, **their** efforts have been eminently successful.

To some, perhaps a majority of readers, these aver- ments will seem utterly preposterous and destitute of all

foundation, fit only to be characterized as the mere utter-
ances of a theorist and one-idea enthusiast. But let us
see what evidence there is on this subject.

And first may be cited the views of the late Henry C.
Carey of Philadelphia, who stands in relation to the modern doctrine of "protection" very much the same as the
Prophet Mahomet does to the religion of Islam. Mr.
Carey expressed the opinion, over and over again, that
the interests of the United States — material and moral —
would be greatly benefited if the Atlantic could be converted into an impassable ocean of fire, and also that a
prolonged war between Great Britain and the United
States would be one of the best possible things which
could happen to promote the industrial independence
and development of the latter country. Of course this
was only another way of saying that ships engaged in the
ocean transport of passengers and merchandise are curses
and nuisances, and that, the sooner they and the trade
which gives them occupation are done away with, the
better for this country. It was a re-indorsement and re-
affirmation of the Chinese policy of hostility to foreigners
and all things foreign, when the Chinese themselves,
after centuries of experience, are proposing to do away
with it.

Horace Greeley also taught substantially the same doctrine to the day of his death. Thus to all who have
rejoiced at the great domestic prosperity which during the
years 1878–81 resulted primarily from the large foreign

demand at good prices for our agricultural products, the following quotation from "The New York Semi-Weekly Tribune" of April 8, 1870, is commended for consideration : —

"When a railroad brings artisans to the door of the farmer, it is a blessing. When it takes the wheat, the flesh, the corn, and the cotton to a distant manufacturing centre, a locomotive is an exhauster : its smoke is a black flag, and its whistle is the scream of an evil genius."

Now, if this doctrine is correct, then the country has no worse enemies than its great railroad constructors and administrators. The men who are stretching Mr. Greeley's black flag over every landscape, and filling the ears of the whole nation with the screams of demons, who have made it possible for the most ordinary mechanic in New England to transport, at the cost of one day's wages, a year's subsistence in bread and meat a thousand miles, or from Chicago to Boston, ought forthwith to be hunted down and subjected to speedy and exemplary punishment. According to this doctrine, furthermore, the country needs no ships for ocean transport, and to seek to promote their construction and employment by subsidies is certainly akin to a crime. We ought also to grow no more wheat, corn, and cotton, raise no more cattle, pack no more pork, and barrel no more petroleum, than are needed for our absolute domestic necessities. Again : in an interview with the late Mr. Greeley, in the summer of 1872, when he was a candidate for the Presidency, he said, "If I could have my way, I would impose a duty of $100 on every ton of pig-iron imported into the United States, and make the rate unchangeable for twenty years. That, sir, is my idea of what our tariff should be." But the plain meaning of this was (if Mr. Greeley was in his right mind), that he would by law prevent ships engaged in ocean transport from obtaining any profitable employment whatever.

But, barbarous and repulsive as are these doctrines and teachings of Messrs. Carey and Greeley, there is even something more singular to be reported. Thus the University of Pennsylvania, which claims to rank among the first educational institutions of the country, openly teaches to its students that it is not expedient that the United States should have any foreign commerce ; that, if there were no other reason for discouraging commerce, the demoralizing effects of a seafaring life would be quite sufficient, and that it would be much better to hang a man than allow him to become a sailor. In confirmation of these seemingly incredible statements, attention is asked to the following quotations from Thompson's "Social Science and National Economy," the text-book for instruction in economic science at present used in the university referred to. In it the author declares (p. 229), "the amount of a nation's foreign commerce the worst possible test of its general prosperity ; " and (p. 222), that "commerce between distant points is an undesirable thing, as open to the exercise of tyrannizing power by traders and their combinations;" and that (p. 228), "if there were no other reasons for the policy which seeks to reduce foreign commerce to a minimum, a sufficient one would be found in the effect on the human material it employs," as if a life on the broad ocean were more demoralizing than an underground existence in the pits and shafts of a coal-mine. "Bentham thought," continues our author, "the worst possible use that could be made of a man was to hang him : a worse still is to make a common sailor of him." And all this in a country whose foreign trade, exports and imports, for the fiscal year 1881, exceeded a thousand six hundred millions of dollars ($1,675,024,318), and which considers the maintenance of a navy and the constant service of a force of 8,000 seamen as essential to its safety !

And again : what could be more audacious than the adoption and indorsement a few years ago, by a leading citizen of Philadelphia, — the president of the so-called "American Industrial League," — of the following lines, which he prefaced as text and motto to an article in "The Atlantic Monthly" on "International Trade"? —

> "Having the power, you have the right:
> One asks but what you've got, not how?
> Talk not to me of navigation ;
> For war, and trade, and piracy, —
> These are a trinity inseparable."

We say "audacious;" for there is no other term which
so fitly characterizes the efforts of a man of high culture
and social position to put the whole body of thought and
action of the community directly across the path of modern civilization, and who, in this latter half of the nineteenth century, uses the words which Goethe puts into
the mouth of Mephistopheles, — or the Devil, — to help
strengthen an argument of his own, that trade and commerce are in all respects equivalent to "war and piracy."

Again: in a debate in the United States House of
Representatives, March 4, 1882, on the features of our
existing consular system, the chairman of the Committee
on Appropriations, Representative Hiscock, of the great
commercial State of New York, admitted that the system
was "complex and to some extent cumbersome," and "an
obstruction to the importation of foreign commodities."
And for the latter reason the speaker declared himself in
favor of its continuance ; for, he continued, " I am unable
to see how, when you relieve the commerce of the country of the weight and burden of the consular system,
you are not to that extent abating the protection which is
given to our industries."   He did not, however, add, what
the reader would do well to bear in mind, that the
existing tariff of the United States (1882) averages more
than 40 per cent on all dutiable importations over and
above the protective obstructions created by our consular
system.

Now, the minds of all this school of economists are

perfectly clear in **respect** to the ideas which they desire to inculcate **and the policy they wish to carry out in the** United States. They are not men who use words without meaning and signification. **They do not believe in inter-** national commerce. **They do not believe in ships. They** **want none** of them. They think **a** man had **better be** hung than engage in ocean transport. They do **not in-** corporate these views into party platforms; for their in- stinct tells them that the people will not stand very much of such talk, and that any man or party that openly in- dorses them would be politically condemned. But they have accomplished indirectly what they would not dare to strive for directly. They have put laws upon our statute- books, and still maintain them there, which practically forbid American manufacturers, agriculturists, and mer- chants from receiving the products of other nations in exchange (payment) for their own ; which say, in fact, to **the** Chilian, "We want to sell you our cotton fabrics and agricultural implements, but you shall not sell us your copper;" and to the producers in the Argentine States, Australia, and the Cape of Good Hope, "We want to sell you clothing, boots and shoes, paints, oils, and gunpowder, and we know we can do so cheaper than any or all other nations ; but we won't buy the prin- cipal product — wool — which you have got to sell (pay with) in return." Now, ships, as was long ago pointed **out, are** the children and not the parents, the effect and not the cause, of commerce ; and so long as we maintain a commercial policy that seeks to interrupt, restrict, or prevent commerce with other nations, so long the ships will not come back to us ; for their employment must be limited, even if they were placed at our wharves as free gifts.

How we Trade with South America.

In proof of this, let us take one of many illustrations that are available. At present the European steamship service with South America comprises British, French, German, and Italian lines, with more than one hundred steamers, making an average of twenty-three monthly trips each way. In 1876 an enterprising firm in Boston, familiar with the shipping business, and desirous of participating in this large South American trade, established a line of steamers to run regularly between Boston and Valparaiso. The ships were built in England, the capital invested in them was American ; but their registry was in London, and they carried the British flag, and were commanded by a British captain. After two years' experience the line was discontinued ; and the United States has now (1882) no regular steam communication with South America, or any direct way of reaching any of its ports. The main reason for the discontinuance of the Boston line was as follows : There was no difficulty at the outset on outgoing cargoes ; as there was, and still is, a demand in Chili for a supply of American farm products, cotton fabrics, machinery, hardware, etc. But ships, to be profitable, must earn freights both going to and returning from a market. Now, the chief commodities that Chili has to pay for or give in return for our products are copper and copper-ores, and wool. But the tariff on the importation of copper is wholly prohibitory, and on wool nearly so ; only one hundred and twenty-five dollars' worth of un-manufactured copper having been imported from all countries in 1879, and about two and a half tons of ore. The consequence was, that these Boston steamers, in order to obtain a return cargo from Chili, were obliged to take freight of wool and copper for Liverpool, and trans-ship it in bond at Boston ; and such a method of doing business proved to be unprofitable. Added to this, the vessels employed were found, after experience, to be not so well suited to the requirements of the trade as was at first expected. Commenting on this venture, one of the partners to it, in a recent letter, writes as follows : —

"The copper product of Chili now nearly all goes to England, where it is manufactured, and distributed all over the world. There is no doubt in our minds that the United States would by this time have possessed nearly all this copper trade, had it not been for the duty imposed about fifteen years ago, which has had the effect to enormously enrich a few copper-producers at Lake Superior, at the expense of the rest of the country, which consumes their production, or rather a part of it only, as they now export about one-quarter the production, and sell it at five cents less per pound than consumers here have to pay for the same copper.

"We have no doubt that the reduction of the duty on copper to a figure that would still allow the Lake Superior mines a fair profit, would so increase our trade with Chili as to permit a profitable business for steamers, and we should pay for all the copper imported with our manufactures of cotton, iron, wood, etc."

As further illustrating how the present tariff policy cripples the use of ships, and shuts us out from the ocean carrying trade in a way that a repeal of navigation, local tax, pilotage, and other similar laws cannot remedy, let us further trace the incidents of this Chilian copper business. Chili now exports about $17,500,000 of copper and copper products. It nearly all goes in British ships, which, loaded in the first instance with the merchandise which Chili wants, — i.e., cotton goods (average $55,000,000 per annum), hardware, paints, paper, machinery, guns, etc., — sail for Valparaiso, earning an outward freight ; arriving in Chili, the cargo unloaded is replaced with another cargo of copper-ores or wool, and the ships return to England, earning homeward freights. Profitable employment is thus given to many British ships, and an explanation in great part afforded of the continued supremacy of the British commercial marine, which strengthens and increases just in proportion as trade increases. Arriving in England, the copper-ores are sold to the copper-smelters at Swansea, in the southeast of England; who, in converting them into mercantile forms, employ English labor, English capital, English railway service, and consume large quantities of English coal. Smelted into ingots, rolled into sheets, or converted into yellow metal or brass, the Chilian copper is finally sold to whoever in the world wants to buy, — and all the world always does want to buy copper under some conditions, — and out of the proceeds of the sale the Swansea smelter pays himself, pays the cotton-spinner, the ship-owner, the coal-miner, the common carrier, and all others concerned ; the movement, as a whole, being in the nature of a great circle of transactions, in every one of which some profit accrues to English capital, and some opportunity is afforded to English labor. But in this great and special circle of production and exchange American capital and labor find no place.

To cap the climax of this curious chapter of our commercial policy, consider now how the American ship-builder and ship-owner supplies himself with copper. English yellow metal, made in part out of copper produced in the United States, and sold at a less price than the American producer will sell to the American consumer, is admitted free of duty if used on American vessels not engaged in the coastwise trade ; while copper and copper ore, out of which the same yellow metal could be made, is not allowed to be brought into the country by reason of the excessive duty imposed on its importation. Could there be any thing in legislation more supremely foolish and ridiculous?

Something of an approximate measurement of the extent of this Chilian business — which is only a fraction of the total South American trade which we have

declined to **participate in, or** rather, which we will not
allow our merchants and ships to attempt to participate in
— may be obtained from the fact, that out of an entrance
and clearance into Valparaiso, in 1877, of 827 steamships
and 1,319 sailing-vessels, representing a **total of** 1,447,368
tons, the United States was represented **by** 68 sailing-
vessels only.

*Tariff Reform essential to the Restoration and Develop-
ment of Shipping* **Interests.**

A radical reform of **our whole tariff** system and policy
is therefore the one great essential for the restoration of
our shipping and our ocean carrying trade.   We have got
to recognize the fact, that it is our present absurd protective policy that has made it impossible to maintain our
status as a commercial nation upon the ocean.   We have
got to recognize the fact that the present pressing necessity of the United States is extended markets for the
continually increasing surplus of our products, — mechanical, mining, and fishing, as well as agriculture, —
that for obtaining such markets ships controlled by and
employed in exclusively American interests are essential
instrumentalities; but that **such** markets will not and
can not be obtained, or a **national** commercial marine
find a basis **for growth, or even** existence, so long as
we restrict by law the producers of this country from
freely exchanging **the** products of their labor with the
products of the **labor of** the producers of other coun-

tries. We have got to recognize the principle **that all**
trade is essentially barter, product being exchanged for
product ; that in order to sell **we must** buy, and in order
to buy we must sell ; that he who won't buy can't sell,
and he who won't sell can't buy ; and that just in proportion as buying or selling, or the exchange of products,
is restricted, to just the same extent the necessity **of**
having instrumentalities of exchange is diminished.

The advocates of the maintenance of the extreme protective system always endeavor to avoid and befog this
phase of the subject under consideration, because they
know full well that an examination of it will at once
expose the fallacy of **the** scheme of attempting to revive
the merchant marine of the United States by a system **of**
subsidies ; for if we are to maintain **a** policy which in
effect proclaims that the United States alone of all the
nations of the world is, and intends to be as far as possible, independent of all foreign trade, what do we want
with ships ? It is also popular with this school of economists, to ridicule our export business as of little account.
" Why," said one of their representatives, **at the Boston**
Shipping Convention in 1880, " we **only export one-tenth**
of our agricultural products;" **but he omitted to men-**
tion that this one-tenth amounted in that same year to
$655,000,000 **in value, on which an ocean** freight reck-
oned at 5 per **cent would have** amounted to over $32,-
000,000. Why **was not the** question asked him, " How
far would this sum have supplied the place of subsidies?"

But, in place of that, the declaration of the speaker was received with great applause, as if it was a matter of congratulation that we exported so little. No one, furthermore, pointed out to the convention that an ability to find a market abroad for this one-tenth of the product determines whether there shall be any profit realized on the other nine-tenths which we market at home, and also whether there shall be for the whole country prosperity or hard times.

Under such circumstances, furthermore, how perfectly puerile it is to suppose, as has recently been done by the representative of the State Department at Washington, that foreign commerce — on which ships engaged in foreign trade must subsist — can be extended under the present tariff by authorizing consuls to act as agents for our manufacturing and commercial firms, or by establishing more direct postal communication with various countries, as, for example, South America! What can consuls accomplish so long as our tariff policy discourages commercial intercourse? Suppose we establish a weekly direct mail with South America, and this mail brings increased orders for United States produce. In what manner are the South Americans to pay for such orders and sales? The Boston experience with Chili shows that they cannot do it with a great part of what South America produces and has to sell. With drafts on England? And, if by drafts, then those drafts have got to be represented by South American exports to England

and not to the **United States.** Can such a trade as this attain any magnitude? Can it warrant the subsidizing of any steamship company?

Conclusion.

From this review, it must **be evident that no one meas-**ure will arrest the decay of American shipping, bring back prosperity to our ocean carrying trade, or revive the **industry** of ship-building in this country. The field of reform to be entered upon is a very large one; the number of details which are to be attended to are numerous; but reform nevertheless is both possible and practicable if the American people desire and will it.

The *first* thing to be done is, then, to educate the people up to a full understanding of the subject.

Second, We must repeal our navigation laws, at least to the extent of permitting our navigators and merchants to supply themselves with ships on conditions as favorable as are enjoyed by their competitors, who are the merchants and sailors of all other maritime nations. There is no other way in which we can supply our needs in respect to ships so speedily. **Grant to** the subsidy scheme all that its friends claim for it, and it will be years before any considerable **results will accrue** from its adoption.

Third, If we are to build ships in the United States as cheaply as they can be built by other nations, — and unless we can do so the ships we may build will never be voluntarily bought or used by our own citizens or any others, — our ship-builders must have their materials for construction as cheap as the builders with whom they are to compete. Either allow the importation free of duty of all the material and stores that enter into the construction and equipment of ships, or reduce the tariff. So long as the business of constructing iron steamships has to bear the burden of high prices consequent on protective duties averaging 40 per cent, it cannot compete with like industries in free-trade countries. There is no possibility of evading this conclusion.

Fourth, If foreign competing maritime nations do not subject their ships to local taxation, the United States evidently cannot afford to do so. The continuance of such a discrimination against our merchant marine of itself and alone may, and probably will, be sufficient to prevent its resuscitation in face of a foreign competition exempt from similar burdens. Whether Congress, under the power conferred upon it by the constitution "to regulate commerce," can exempt as instrumentalities of commerce vessels engaged in foreign or inter-state carrying trade from all forms of local — state or municipal — taxation, is, however, an open question. The decisions of the United States Supreme Court on this subject look both ways.[1]

---

[1] The following is a summary of the most important of these decisions, and the inferences deducible from them. In the case of Weston *vs.* the city of Charleston (2 Peters, 449), the Court, through Chief Justice Marshall, said, " The power to tax involves the power to destroy ; " and, " If the right

Fifth, Abolish compulsory pilotage, and reduce the fees for pilotage by law so that they shall not be in excess of those charged in British and other European ports.

---

to impose a tax exists, it is a right which in its nature acknowledges no limits." Once concede, therefore, to the States the right to tax the instrumentalities of inter-state or foreign commerce in any degree, and you concede, it may be claimed, to the States the right to say there shall be no inter-state or foreign commerce : for the right to impose one per cent of taxation involves the right to impose 100 per cent; or, in other words, the right to tax at all involves the right to prevent. Again : in definition of the extent of the power of Congress to regulate commerce, the Supreme Court in the case of Weston *vs.* the State of Missouri (Otto 1, pp. 275–283) said, " Commerce is a term of the largest import. It comprehends intercourse for the purpose of trade in any and all its forms, including the transportation, purchase, sale, and exchange of commodities between the citizens of one country and the citizens and subjects of other countries, and between the citizens of different States. The power to regulate it embraces all the instruments by which such commerce may be conducted."

Justice Story ruled that the power given to Congress to regulate commerce with foreign nations and among the States has been deemed exclusive from the nature and objects of the power and the necessary implications growing out of its exercise. And on another occasion the full bench held that " whenever subjects, in regard to which a power to regulate commerce is asserted, are in their nature national, or admit of one uniform system or plan of regulation, they are exclusively within the regulating control of Congress."

In the celebrated case of Gibbons *vs.* Ogden, Chief Justice Marshall defined commerce to be not only traffic, but " intercourse between nations and parts of nations in all its branches ; " and he added, " It is regulated by prescribing rules for carrying on that intercourse." Enlarging on this point, he continued, " The subject, the vehicle, the agent, and their various operations, become the objects of commercial regulations." And of late years this idea

Sixth, Repeal the tonnage-tax.

Seventh, Reduce all expenses connected with the hiring or discharge of seamen, consular charges, and the like, to the level or below those imposed by other nations. If,

---

has been so far adopted as to impute to Congress the power to determine the circumstances under which a bridge may be built over a navigable stream; and Congress has also enacted codes regulating in a minute degree the construction, equipment, and navigation of steam-vessels. In the case of the "State Freight Tax" (15 Wallace, 282), the Court through Mr. Justice Strong said, "We recognize fully the power of each State to tax at its discretion its own internal commerce, and the franchises, property, or business of its own corporations, so that inter-state intercourse, trade, or commerce is not embarrassed or restricted. That must remain free." "No State can impose a tax upon freight transported from State to State, or upon the transporter because of such transportation." This decision does not decide that a State may not tax the vehicle or the carriage employed in such transportation; but it is obvious, that would not be permitted to be done indirectly which it was forbidden to do directly.

On the other hand, in the case of Brown *vs.* Maryland (12 Wheaton, 431), Chief Justice Marshall said, "Nothing can be more fallacious than to urge the possible abuse of power by the States, for the purpose of proving that the power has been taken away. Such an argument goes to the destruction of all State power." In the case of the "State Tax on Gross Receipts" (15 Wallace, 293-294), Mr. Justice Strong, in giving the opinion of the Court, said, "No doubt every tax upon personal property, or upon occupations, business, or franchises, affects, more or less, the subjects and the operations of commerce. Yet it is not every thing that affects commerce that amounts to a regulation of it within the meaning of the Constitution. We think it may safely be asserted, that the States have authority to tax the estate, real and personal, of all their corporations, including carrying companies, precisely as they may tax similar property belonging to natural persons and to the same extent. We think also that such taxation may be laid upon a valuation, or may be an excise. It must be admitted that a tax upon any article of per-

however, the decline of American shipping continues
much longer, these reforms will be unnecessary, for there
will be no sailors hired or discharged; and no necessity of

---

sonal property that may become a subject of commerce, or upon any instrument of commerce, affects commerce. If the tax be upon the instrument,
such as a stage-coach, a railroad-car, or a canal or steam boat, its tendency is
to increase the cost of transportation. Still it is not a tax upon transportation or upon commerce, and it has never been seriously doubted that such
a tax may be laid."

The question at issue would therefore seem to be: can local taxation of the
vehicles of commerce be considered as a regulation of the commerce itself?
If it is, then Congress, within the meaning of the Constitution, has exclusive
power to tax that great class of property owned by American citizens which
is or may be employed in the foreign trade. The sphere of the application of this power admits also of the following illustrations: "A boat
owned in Maine, and employed exclusively in carrying passengers between
Portland and Eastport, would be liable to tax according to the laws of that
State; but, the moment it extended its trips to St. John, the Maine authorities would lose all rights in it. If such a case were taken to the Supreme
Court, that would have to be its decision to harmonize with those of the
past." Let it be admitted further, that Congress can exempt vessels running
between the United States and foreign countries from local taxation by
States of the Federal Union, and the exercise of this prerogative would
seem to embrace and carry with it the right to forbid the States from taxing
vessels or vehicles — i.e., railroad-cars — employed as instrumentalities for
the transaction of inter-state commerce. The best way out of the difficulty,
pending action of the United States Supreme Court, would therefore seem to
be for all the States, recognizing the axiom in taxation, that it is not necessary to tax every thing to tax equitably, to exempt vessels from direct taxation; or, apart from any economic principle, follow the example of Pennsylvania, New York, and Massachusetts, and exempt, as a matter of simple
expediency, vessels engaged in foreign trade from all direct taxation, leaving,
if needs be, only their income liable to taxation.

invoking the co-operation of consuls, for there will be no ships engaged in foreign trade.

Eighth, Reform the tariff, and the natural resources of our country and the intelligence of our people are such, that, with the reduction of the burden of taxes and prices consequent on low rates of duty, we shall regain in the next twenty years more than we have lost in the last twenty, and become the first maritime nation of the world.

Ninth, Without resorting to the artificial expedient of subsidies and bounties, let Congress assimilate steamships and railroads in their treatment, to the extent of paying steamships for carrying the mails of the United States good compensation, — as good as the government now pays railways for performing similar service.[1]

---

[1] The United States now pays the steam-lines carrying her European mails five francs per kilogramme for letters, and 50 centimes per kilogramme for papers; these rates having been fixed by the International Postal Congress. Practically, this amounts to an average of about $600 per trip. Returning from Liverpool, the sum is a trifle greater, because England pays for the detention of the steamers at Queenstown. All the lines running from New York to Liverpool carry the mails at these rates, except the National. The White Star, Inman, and Cunard carry the Liverpool mails to New York. The lines running between New York, Havre, Antwerp, and Hamburg get a similar rate fixed by the International Postal Congress. An American line running to the same ports should obviously receive the same compensation, the conditions of safety and expedition being satisfactory; for the Post-Office Department could legitimately follow no other rule than to get its service done at the lowest cost possible.

INDEX.

---

www.ingramcontent.com/pod-product-compliance
Lightning Source LLC
Chambersburg PA
CBHW030318270326
41926CB00010B/1421